Dawn & David,

It is always a pleasure
working with you. I look
forward to working with you
and your friends real soon.

Ron Dunlap 3/31/10

What others are saying about this book:

"There are very few books on the topic of real estate investing that you can read, put down, and immediately start investing with confidence. *Push Button Investing* is one of those books."

Todd Duncan
New York Times best selling author and speaker

"*Push Button Investing* is not a get-rich-quick scheme. It is a calculated system that generates wealth over time."

David Jaffe
mortgage loan originator

"Ron Draluck relies on common sense rather than an accounting formula. It is so easy that anyone can benefit."

Jeff Lake
mortgage loan originator

"In a world of 'how to' books, *Push Button Investing* stands tall above the rest. As a mortgage loan officer and branch manager, I would highly recommend this book as a must read for those in the mortgage or real estate business, as well as anyone wanting simple, yet effective, tools to be successful in acquiring investment real estate."

Linda Davidson
senior loan officer/branch manager
direct endorsement underwriter

"Getting started is the hardest part. With the *Push Button Investing* system, it's easy to get started. You have all the key pieces to close the deal and all the support services to keep it going."

Larry Conn
real estate appraiser

"Following Ron Draluck's proven strategy was the best financial move I ever made!"

T. Darrell Albright
VP of sales

"Retirement in less than 10 years is my new goal and Ron Draluck's *Push Button Investing* system will really make it happen."

Paul Merriman
real estate agent

"Real estate investing is a necessary part of any successful investment portfolio. *Push Button Investing* allows anyone to acquire and own real estate with an unlimited growth potential."

Danny Cargal
real estate agent

PUSH BUTTON
INVESTING
IN REAL ESTATE

PUSH BUTTON
INVESTING
IN REAL ESTATE

The Safe, Systematic Way To Create
Wealth In Residential Real Estate

Ron Draluck

PUSH BUTTON INVESTING IN REAL ESTATE
The Safe, Systematic Way to Create Wealth
in Residential Real Estate

by Ron Draluck

Copyright © 2007 by Ron Draluck
Push Button Investing™

Published by:
Book Marketing Solutions, LLC
10300 E. Leelanau Court
Traverse City, MI 49684
orders@BookMarketingSolutions.com
www.BookMarketingSolutions.com

Printed in the United States of America

Draluck, Ron.
   Push button investing in real estate : the safe, systematic way to
   create wealth in residential real estate / Ron Draluck. -- Traverse
   City, Mich : Book Marketing Solutions, 2207.

       p. ; cm.
       (Push button investing)
       ISBN-13: 978-0-9790834-7-1
       ISBN-10: 0-9790834-7-8
       Includes bibliographical references.

       1. Real estate investment--Handbooks, manuals, etc.
   2. Investments--Handbooks, manuals, etc. 3. Finance, Personal--
   Handbooks, manuals, etc. 4. Real estate business--United States--
   Handbooks, manuals, etc. I. Title.

HD1382.5 .D73 2007
332.63/24--dc22   0706

This book is available at:
www.ReadingUp.com

DEDICATION

This book is dedicated to my lovely bride, Bonnie, and my two sons, Mark and Ross.

ACKNOWLEDGEMENT

I would like to thank Kate Wilson for helping me envision Push Button Investing and inspiring me to write this book.

CONTENTS

How and Why I Got Started
What Is Push Button Investing?

Land Ownership Is the Oldest Form of Wealth
Real Estate Is More Tangible Than Stocks and Bonds
Fundamentally Sound Companies Can Drop in Value
More Real Estate Can Be Acquired through Leveraging
Investment Real Estate Offers Dividends and Capital Gains

The Real Estate Boom
An Improving Economy
Interest Rates
It Takes Courage to Be Successful at Anything

You Do Not Need the Amenities That You Are Used To
Serving a Purpose

PART FOUR: Managing Your Properties

FOREWORD

There is a wide array of books available on the topic of real estate investing. Most are filled with either pie-in-the-sky promises that materialize only for a very small percentage of readers, or oversimplified strategies that require readers to guess, continue learning on their own, or purchase the missing pieces that make the formula work.

There are very few books on the topic of real estate investing that you can read, put down, and immediately start investing with confidence. *Push Button Investing* is one of those books.

One of the things our studies showed us during the writing of *High*

Trust Selling was that people generally don't implement what they can't fully comprehend. If there is even a slight incongruity or deficiency to a proposed course of action in the pages of a book, the majority of readers will fail to apply it to their lives—despite how helpful and how necessary it might seem. Ron has made sure this will not happen to you.

In the pages of this book, you will find that every piece of his strategy is well-explained, easy to understand, and properly placed into the context of the bigger picture—that you will, when you finish reading, be able to begin the process of investing in real estate right away. Additionally, about one-quarter into the book you will find yourself wondering how something so potentially life-changing could be so easy.

Real estate and real estate investing have been a part of my professional life for more than two decades, and I have experienced the challenges to being successful in the industry. This is why I can say with certainty that *Push Button Investing* is a distinctive book. It allows you to build an investment portfolio and make money in real estate whether you have been at it for over twenty-five years like me or have never bought a single home. It isn't too much to say that Ron makes real estate investing as easy as pushing buttons. This is a book I wish I had read when I was twenty, so I urge you to digest it as quickly as you can. You'll soon see what I mean.

Todd Duncan
New York Times best selling author and speaker

PART ONE

INVESTING IN REAL ESTATE

Introduction

*"Achieving wealth is as easy
as pushing a button."*

Ron Draluck

How and Why I Got Started

I grew up in a real estate family. The interest in real estate began with my grandfather, who owned more than 150 single family investment homes. He was able to buy houses during the Depression for a few hundred dollars each, and he hired a team of people to help him manage those investment homes. Years later, my grandfather sold those properties for an average of $50,000 each and amassed a large amount of cash from his gains.

My father is an active commercial real estate agent who has been in business for more than 40 years. His specialty is apartments. Before my father begins to work with new clients, he insists that they either be experienced at managing apartments or have a reputable property manager assist them while they own the property. His investors always come back to buy from him again and again because of the huge profit they achieve upon the sale of their properties.

I have been in the residential mortgage business now for over two decades. During this time, I have also been a real estate investor. My first deal was an investment in a small apartment complex for $10,000 per unit. My partner was an experienced property manager. We bought in a high growth area, which allowed us to sell the complex for $30,000 per unit within a three-year period.

By adapting the same fundamentals that my family used, I have been able to profitably invest in commercial and residential real estate. In addition to my personal experience, I have witnessed home buyers for whom I wrote mortgages, profit in a very short period of time. In many cases, not only did they profit quickly, but their returns were extremely high when compared to their initial investments. After experiencing and then observing this type of success, I began to discern a pattern of profitability that can be bottled and duplicated. Best of all, it's straightforward and relatively hassle-free.

Most people I come in contact with believe they should invest in real estate. They hear about the success of others and would like that success for themselves. There is usually only one thing stopping them: fear. They are afraid they will lose their investment; or they're afraid of losing their tenant; or inheriting a property that requires excessive repairs; or renting to someone who ruins the property; or perhaps having to deal with any one of a list of issues they've heard about that just isn't worth the trouble.

I talk with potential investors—well-meaning, fiscally wise people—every day, and I am convinced that these fears, while possible, are rarely substantiated in well-thought-out investment scenarios. More often than not, they are like the grade school rumor about the haunted house on the hill. Everyone believes it's true until someone actually knocks on the door and discovers the sweet, older couple who's lived there for decades.

If you dare to knock on the door of real estate investment, I have a system to that removes the worry and fear from the process. It is called *Push Button Investing*™.

What Is Push Button Investing?

By trade, I am a mortgage loan officer. I have been in the same profession for over twenty-four years, but about five years ago I realized that my job lacked meaning. I followed the same routine day in and day out, and something needed to change. I helped my clients obtain mortgage financing for the purchase or refinance of residential real estate. While I was able to fulfill their immediate needs, this role, over time, did little else for me. How exciting could it be after so many years?

Then I heard about business coaching for individuals who wanted to enhance their careers. I inquired about it, thinking a coach could put more zing into my workday. I subsequently hired Kate and we immediately went to work.

One of the first goals she had me identify was my purpose. Why do I do what I do? How does that affect my well-being? How can I successfully help my clients and feel fulfilled at the same time?

After a couple of weeks, I came up with my answer. My purpose is, "to create wealth for my clients through home ownership." It sounded great. It was meaningful. It made me feel I was giving something back and producing more than a paycheck.

During my next coaching session, Kate asked me a more difficult question: "How are you going to create wealth for your clients through home ownership?" The purpose was there—helping people create wealth—but there was nothing tangible to back up my objective. Had I actually done that? I hadn't kept track. I thought long and hard, and decided to look for past scenarios in my mortgage career in which clients actually made a lot of money with homes I helped them purchase.

I immediately remembered a couple who could barely scrape together their 5 percent down payment, $7,500, to purchase their first home. One-and-a-half years later, they sold their home and walked away with $75,000 in profit. In 18 months, the equity in their home grew tenfold. This was an incredible return, and I was immediately grateful at the realization that I was part of their story.

I also remembered another couple to whom I lent money. Ben and his wife, Beth, bought a house in the same area as the first couple, also with little money down. After a couple of years, they refinanced their home and pulled cash out for future investments. They used some of the cash from the refinance to make a down payment on a rental house in the same area. Six months later, they bought a second rental house. As it turned out, this area of town was an ideal rental market and the rents they could demand enabled the couple to net between $400 and $500 in profit (income after mortgage and maintenance) each month.

Although Ben and Beth were interested in monthly income, they were simultaneously accumulating an incredible amount of equity in their two rental houses, which was even better. They knew a good thing when they saw it and continued seizing the opportunity. Now the couple owns more than fifteen homes. Their monthly profit is so good that Ben was able to quit his day job and instead manages their real estate full time.

Another couple that I helped followed the same route. They refinanced their home and invested their equity in rental properties. When I checked, I found that they too now own twelve to fifteen houses, in any given year, and are doing quite well. I continued looking for comparable situations and discovered that

I had more clients with similar characteristics, who were doing the same thing in other areas of town.

While I hadn't actually taught these people to invest, I believed I had at least started them on the right path by helping them buy their first home. This felt good. Still, I couldn't say that I had fulfilled my purpose of helping people create wealth through home ownership because I had only assisted these people with their mortgages. What they accomplished beyond my service was not something for which I could take credit.

Nevertheless, during this search back through my career, I became so impressed with what my clients had been able to accomplish that I contracted to buy an investment house myself. This investment was special because I was doing it without the advice or expertise of my experienced family members. I felt so proud and was certain the results would be positive.

Then, suddenly, I broke out in a cold sweat. It dawned on me that I did not live or work near this home. Who was going to manage it? Who was going to make repairs? Who was going to show the property to potential tenants? I had no desire to do any of that. Then I had an idea. Why couldn't Ben manage the property for me? He was already managing multiple properties of his own.

After a phone call, we reached an agreement. Ben would manage my investment home for a fee of the first month's rent and $100 a month. To me, that was a bargain. As it turned out, my profit after the house payment and Ben's management fee was still $350 a month.

I watched my successful investment for a year and then bought another house. I had been involved in real estate all of my life but never found anything as easy as this. Additionally, I began to realize that my purpose was gaining a foundation. I finally had something tangible to offer my clients.

If I could bottle this real estate investment strategy, I could truly "create wealth for my clients through home ownership." By doing so, I would be living out my purpose, and the extra mortgages would ensure that my staff and I would have plenty of work. Thus was born the *Push Button Investing*™ (PBI) system, which was based on my family's heritage, the investment success of my clients, and my constant desire to add deeper meaning to my career.

The PBI system recognizes two types of real estate investors. The first type is someone who is handy with a hammer and paintbrush. This person does not mind dealing with leasing the property and screening potential tenants. He or she is happy to take phone calls at night and meet contractors at the property for repairs.

The second type of investor is someone who sits at a desk, runs numbers, and determines which properties will provide good returns. Unlike the first type of investor, the second type prefers to leave the hands-on duties to someone else. I am the second type of investor. I concluded that I would rather push the buttons on a calculator and hire someone to handle the maintenance and contract work. My family had always invested this way; we just didn't realize everyone else wasn't doing the same thing.

Regardless of which type of investor you want to be, by using the PBI strategy, you can achieve surprising success without the effort and anxiety you have probably come to expect from investing in real estate. Hiring a PBI team removes the worry and hassle by helping you properly locate, finance, and manage quality properties to ensure a solid return on your investments. Whether you are an experienced investor or just starting out, this book will help you put together a team of three professionals—a mortgage planner, a property locator, and a property manager—in order to achieve Push Button success, the same kind of success that my clients achieve today.

Bill, a colleague of mine, owns more than twenty properties. Although he is a successful real estate investor, he spends too much time managing his properties. He does not have enough time to spend with his family or on his mortgage business. We recently spoke about his dilemma and I suggested that he add a property manager to his team. He took my advice and the results were impressive. I was happy to hear him say, "I can't believe that I didn't think about this sooner. My time has been freed up significantly and I can expand my real estate investing with no additional effort." The same can be true of your investment efforts.

In the end, my objective for you is the same as it was for Bill: I want to help you create wealth through home ownership. I'm grateful that I have identified the tools to accomplish this, and I want to share them with you.

PBI NOTES

»Push Button Investing. This is a real estate investment system that has worked for me. I challenge you to try it.

»To receive a free copy of my online newsletter about real estate investing, go to my Web site at pushbuttoninvesting.com

Buying Real Estate as an Alternative Investment

"All great things are simple."

Winston Churchill

Land Ownership Is the Oldest Form of Wealth

Before there were high rises, office buildings, apartment buildings, shopping malls, strip mall centers, or single family houses, there was land. Land is the simplest and oldest form of real estate. On it, you can grow crops for food, you can raise animals, and you can build shelter. For thousands of years, land was one of the greatest indicators of wealth. Wars have been waged over land; people have fought for it and died for it. Lives and families were uprooted so people could board ships or travel miles on horseback or foot for a chance to own land.

Real estate became the original "American Dream." Many

immigrants journeyed to America for the opportunity to become landowners. In the 1500s, our country was sparsely populated. For the cost of the registration, you could stake a claim for your own land, and many did. Some of these original landowners became the wealthiest people in America.

A few centuries later, our country faced the Depression. At that time, many wealthy people lost everything. Yet many of those who weathered the extreme adversity of the Depression were farmers. Their land was not lost when the stock market crashed. Furthermore, they could grow food on their own land, and food became a commodity that could be used in trade for other products.

It's for good reason that people have always aspired to own real estate. Many methods of building wealth have come and gone, but owning land has remained a constant. In fact, you will find that the richest people in the world all have some portion of their wealth in real estate—it is a fundamental pillar of investment strategy. That's because land does not disappear. It is the most stable, tangible form of wealth available to us.

Real Estate Is More Tangible Than Stocks and Bonds

Because it has been made very easy to do, many people own stocks and bonds.[1] By the turn of the century, approximately half of all U.S. households had money in these investments. But what do you get in return for investing in stocks and bonds? You get a piece of paper representing a company. The company is then responsible for earning a profit. The owner of this piece of paper (the stockholder) relies on the board of directors and corporate management to make decisions to keep the company profitable. When determining whether to invest, the only facts that the investor has to go on are the history of the company and the track record of the management. You can't count on the company's future performance or the success of its leadership.

Fundamentally Sound Companies Can Drop in Value

Buying stock is a way to own a portion of a large, profitable company. This makes stock ownership extremely popular. Unfortunately, the percentage of ownership most investors acquire is very small—typically less than 1 percent. Add to this the reality that there is no guarantee the company will survive, and you can see that there may be sounder investments. What if there is mismanagement? What if there is an accounting scandal? What if there is a misrepresentation? The answers to these questions are evident in recent events.

Enron was a mighty company that looked like a great investment on paper. Many people put thousands of their hard-earned dollars into the company. They trusted the track record and the effectiveness of the leadership. Today, Enron doesn't exist.

It went under due to reasons beyond its stockholders' control. Stockholders relied on management to make good decisions and abide by all standard accounting guidelines, but management failed them. The same holds true for Arthur Andersen. Once considered one of the most conservative and reliable accounting firms in the world, today it no longer exists.

On a larger scale, many people's stock holdings lost substantial value during the tech debacle. At one time, any company with a "dot-com" next to its name had a significant run-up. With the potential for lucrative, short-term returns, more and more people were lured into stock investing. We now know what happened to many of those portfolios when the majority of those companies lost their value.

I agree that company stock can be a great investment. However, small investors—which most of us are—typically have no control over the success of the company into which they invest, and therefore, no control over the success of their investment. Owners of real estate, as you will learn, have far greater control.

More Real Estate Can Be Acquired through Leveraging

Real estate is one of the few investments that can be acquired without spending much money up front. Depending on occupancy—whether you will live there or lease to a tenant— you can acquire a house with as little as a 0 to 10 percent down payment. As an investor, this is a great opportunity.

Suppose that you buy a home for $200,000 with a 10 percent down payment. That means your initial investment is $20,000. You have purchased this home with leverage. You bought a $200,000 asset with only $20,000 from your bank account. Now suppose that the house appreciates in value to $220,000. That means the value has increased by $20,000. In this case, you invested $20,000 and earned $20,000, which means you made a 100 percent return on your investment. You have earned a return on the entire $200,000 but only had to invest $20,000. There are practically no other investments that you can leverage like real estate.

> "Brenda and I have found PBI to be a very effective method of leveraging our investment money. PBI is a great way to make substantial profits from small investments."
>
> *Alan Lewis*
> *director of sales and marketing*

For example, my clients bought a $150,000 home with only $7,500 from their bank account. Yet they walked away with $75,000 plus their initial down payment. They leveraged their investment by spending only 5 percent ($7,500) of the entire purchase price. In this way, they could realize a return on the full price of $150,000. The $75,000 profit on their $7,500 investment enabled them to increase their investment tenfold. That is a 1,000 percent return.

Essentially, leveraging allows you to buy an appreciating asset without paying for it in full. People with a large amount of savings can use leverage to buy a number of properties at a time. But as you will soon see, you don't need a big savings account to begin investing today.

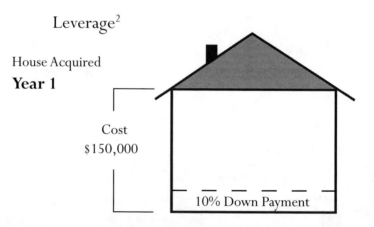

Leverage[2]

House Acquired
Year 1

Cost
$150,000

10% Down Payment

If you bought a $150,000 house with leverage, borrowing 90 percent, your initial investment (down payment) is $15,000.

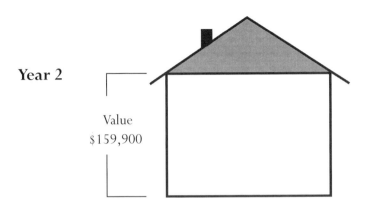

Year 2

Value
$159,900

The house appreciated 6.4 percent in first year. You made $9,900 in one year on your $15,000 investment. That is a 66 percent return.

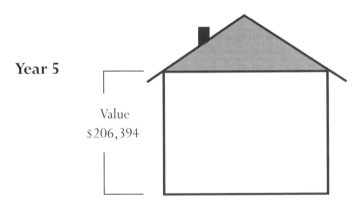

Year 5

Value
$206,394

The house continued to appreciate over a five-year period. You made $56,394 in five years on your $15,000 investment. That is a 376 percent return.

Investment Real Estate Offers Dividends and Capital Gains

Like stocks, a rental property can create a monthly cash flow. This cash flow is similar to stock dividends in that you receive regular, positive income during ownership of the investment.

If, for example, you rent a home to a tenant and the rental profit is $200 per month after the mortgage and expenses have been paid, that's a 12 percent annual dividend on a $20,000 investment. You earn $2,400 per year, divided by your $20,000 investment, which equals an annual return of 12 percent. If your rental income is $400 per month, or $4,800 per year, that's a 24 percent annual dividend on your investment.

The hidden beauty of real estate dividends is that, unlike stock dividends, this monthly income can be sheltered by using expenses such as depreciation. Obviously, it is better to earn income without tax consequences.

There is another similarity between investing in real estate and investing in stocks. Like stocks, investment real estate can provide a profit, or capital gain, when sold (sales price minus the original purchase price equals profit). While both stock and real estate investments may qualify for lower taxes when sold due to capital gains tax treatment, the hidden difference is that only real estate can be sold for a gain without immediate tax consequences.

Tax on the gain from the sale of investment real estate may be completely deferred with what is called a 1031 tax-free exchange. I'll describe this in more detail later, but for now the point is simple. Theoretically, an individual can perpetually buy and sell investment properties without paying taxes. In contrast, the gain from the sale of a stock does not have a tax deferral opportunity.

Although there are many investments you can make with your money that require some risk, few allow you the control and manageability that real estate does. With real estate, you have to rely on someone else's decisions or leadership skill in order to realize a good return. However, if you do your homework and get the right people on your team, a nice return is almost automatic. Best of all, there is always a good investment to be had in any market.

> *"Getting started is the hardest part. With your Push Button Investing system, you make it easy to get started. You have all the key pieces to close the deal and all the support services to keep it going."*
>
> *Larry Conn*
> *appraiser*

PBI NOTES

» Land is the oldest form of wealth. This investment is tried and true. Do not change a winning game.

» Real estate is more tangible than stocks and bonds—you can see it, live on or in it, and change it.

» Fundamentally sound companies can drop in value. As a small-time property owner, you are not susceptible to the challenges and constraints of corporate America.

» Real estate can be acquired through leveraging. It is one of the few remaining investments where you can profit from ownership with only a small initial investment.

» Real estate investment offers favorable tax treatment. Current tax law on real estate provides methods for deferring and even exempting gains realized.

» For more information on real estate investing, go to my Web site at pushbuttoninvesting.com

NOW IS THE TIME TO BUY

"If you could get the courage to begin, you have the courage to succeed."

DavidViscott

The Real Estate Boom

Home ownership in America has become easier to achieve. More people own their homes than ever before. According to a report by the nation's top housing and mortgage economists in the January 10, 2005, issue of *Originator Times*, "the national homeownership rate will rise above today's record level and will most likely exceed 70 percent by 2013." [3]

Lending institutions are working hard to create ways for almost everyone to be able to buy a home, and there is practically no end in sight. According to the February 18, 2005, edition of *The Kiplinger Letter*, "the U.S. will need about two million new homes every year over the next decade just to keep up with growth in the number of new households and to replace aging apartments and houses."[4]

If this is true, the demand for housing will remain strong. That demand will support home prices and contribute to an increase in market values, which makes it an ideal situation for the real estate investor. So now is the time to buy.

An Improving Economy

An improving economy creates more jobs, an increase in eligible home buyers, greater housing demand, and home appreciation. Not only is this the perfect combination for those who want to make money in real estate, but there are many reasons to believe that housing demand and appreciation will continue.

According to an April 11, 2005, *BusinessWeek* article, "besides the good job and income growth associated with a healthy economy, there are other compelling reasons that the market won't soften too much. Baby boomers continue to fuel demand—especially for second homes—and immigrants are increasingly becoming first-time home buyers."[5] That makes the present a good time to invest in real estate.

Interest Rates

Interest rates on mortgages fluctuate and are unpredictable. Although changes in interest rates will affect the payment on your investment home, a rise in interest rates does not make your investment less attractive. As a matter of fact, you can be a successful investor in any interest rate environment.

If you buy an investment property when interest rates are falling, the mortgage payment on your investment home will be lower. Lower payments also create a larger monthly cash flow. A larger cash flow allows you to set money aside in reserves and profit from your investment each month.

Still, investors can be successful when buying real estate during periods of high interest rates. Because the economy is affected by the rise and fall of interest rates, when interest rates are high, the demand for real estate is lower. In an environment where there is less demand, the savvy investor can get a better price on promising real estate. If you are able to buy your investment at a price that is temporarily low, you will set yourself up for an even bigger profit later when you sell.

Another benefit of purchasing investment real estate when interest rates are high is the surplus of renters. As interest rates rise, so do house payments. This decreases the ability of potential homeowners to purchase their own home. As a result, more and more people drop out of the purchase arena and continue to rent. In other words, when home ownership is less affordable, the rental market becomes "hot." Not only do investors have a larger group of renters to choose from, they can also command higher rents.

The point is that whether mortgage interest rates are high or low, now is the time to invest. As an investor, you can succeed in any economic environment.

It Takes Courage to Be Successful at Anything

Many people have dreams of fame and fortune. Some imagine what they could do and what they could buy if they had an unlimited supply of money. Some instead dream of personal success and recognition. Yet, despite all our wishful thinking, there are far more people who never achieve their dreams than those who do. The people who realize their dreams have one particular commonality that makes a huge difference: they have the courage to move forward.

It's hard to believe, but I've found that most people actually have a fear of success. They are worried about how to get started and they are worried about the massive amount of work necessary to maintain their success once they achieve it. To such people, it is easier to remain in their comfort zone, even if it's not the place they would prefer to be.

Fortunately, my son, Mark, realized what it takes to succeed early in his life. I would describe him as a "grade prostitute." In high school, he would do anything within reason to land a good grade on an assignment. He was once assigned a history presentation on the Declaration of Independence. Through his research, he discovered there was a musical production called "1776," which was set during the period of time leading up to the signing of the Declaration. In the play, John Adams had a monologue, and at one point broke out into song and dance. Mark felt that performing this act from the production was perfect for his assignment. (It should be noted that Mark is not in the school drama program.)

When the day came, he dressed up in a triangular hat, puffy shirt, knickers, and other garb of that era. He then proceeded to deliver his speech, and, at just the right moment, he dramatically burst into song before his entire class.

The evening after his performance, I asked him, "Why didn't you just write a report?"

"Dad," he replied, "if you embarrass yourself in front of the class, you will get a good grade."

Mark was right. He got an A. He was nervous and embarrassed, but he felt that if he did something courageous, he would succeed.

I was thinking more about this relationship between success

and courage the other day when a friend of mine, who plays a lot of tennis, came to mind. When he is warming up, he is always more relaxed and takes risky shots that have less chance of landing in bounds. However, when it comes to match play, he hits more conservatively; he plays only the shots he knows will stay in bounds. As a result, his game is less aggressive when it counts. He plays conservatively against more aggressive players and he tends to lose. Although he analyzes the matches, he cannot figure out why he couldn't beat a less-skilled player.

Then one day he employed a coach to help him with his game. The coach told him there was nothing wrong with his ground strokes—he was a good hitter. The problem, the coach said, was that in match play he was unwilling to go for the shots he takes in practice. My friend was so fearful of not winning that he was failing to take the risks necessary to win.

Success in real estate investing is very similar. You must take a chance, knowing that all investments have risk. You must move courageously forward or you will never be in a place to realize great returns.

In this book, I will plainly lay out for you some simple steps necessary for success in real estate investing. It is then your job to decide if you have the courage to take them.

PBI NOTES

» The real estate boom. There will be a housing demand for years to come.

» The ten-year rise in home ownership. More Americans than ever before can afford to buy. This will result in a housing demand. The greater the demand, the more valuable homes become.

» An improving economy. More jobs produce more potential buyers. These new buyers will increase demand. As demand increases, supply will decrease. Real estate investors will benefit.

» Interest rates do not matter. Real estate investment can be profitable in any environment.

» It takes courage to be successful. Don't sit on the sidelines and watch others succeed.

» Go to my Web site at pushbuttoninvesting.com for articles about real estate investment.

THE PUSH BUTTON INVESTING TEAM

*"Nothing is particularly hard
if you divide it up into small jobs."*

Henry Ford

The Team

The strength of the Push Button Investing strategy is in the team you will form. The main objective of a PBI team is to take the fear and hassle out of real estate investing. If everything is taken care of for you, then achieving success is straightforward.

A successful PBI team is comprised of three key members:

1. The mortgage lender
2. The property locator
3. The property manager

An investor who employs an experienced PBI team will have the confidence to move forward and start making money right away.

Later, I will show you how to find and hire each member of your PBI team. For now, let's discuss the general roles they will play and their importance in the overall strategy.

> *"Your team concept allows me to profit without the worry and hassle."*
>
> Bonnie Tager
> stay-at-home mom

The Mortgage Lender

This is the first member of your PBI team. In layman's terms, this is the person who secures a loan for the purchase of your investment homes. He or she should be able to leverage the purchase of your homes by providing the largest mortgage with the lowest possible mortgage payment.

It should be noted that mortgage lending for rental property is more complex than lending on one's primary home. For starters, both the interest rate and the size of the down payment are higher on investment property. Additionally, in many cases, investors purchase a home before a lease is in place. This can make it difficult for the investor to qualify for another mortgage without rental income to offset the mortgage payment. Sometimes mortgage lending guidelines require that the investor have experience in owning real estate. Fully aware of these factors, a good mortgage lender will offer several options to fit your particular situation. There are different parameters for different scenarios, so it is crucial that the lender you choose is well-versed in investment lending as it will greatly simplify your investing process.

The mortgage lender you choose must also be on your side and look out for your interests. While any lender can get a mortgage approved, yours should do more. He or she should ask about your intentions for the investment and then offer advice on financing. What length of time do you plan on owning the property? What is your investment objective? Are you keeping the property for two years, five years, or twenty years? Perhaps you are only going to own the property for six months due to an immediate profit potential. A good lender will want to know the answers to these questions before arranging for financing.

The Property Locator

The second member of your team is the property locator. This person is usually a real estate agent but can also be a non-Realtor. In general, the property locator must know the real estate market where you intend to invest. This person must be able to locate properties in low-cost areas where there is a high *velocity of appreciation*™. Moreover, these properties must be in areas that can easily be leased with top rents. In short, the property locator must know how to survey all aspects of a market so he or she can find the right house for you.

Steve is a property locator I have used in the past. He also is a real estate agent. He knows the market backward and forward, and he only shows properties in areas where he is an expert. If Steve feels a certain unfamiliar area meets the required Push Button Investing characteristics, he will study it first before recommending a purchase for one of his clients, myself included.

Locators like Steve stay on the lookout for areas in town that are in the beginning of their appreciation stage. In many cases, these are in-town properties that were popular decades ago. Eventually though, families passed them over and moved out to the suburbs. Now with the increasing cost of transportation (fuel) and longer work commutes, in-town areas are becoming more desirable and practical. This trend is currently fueling a migration that has stimulated property appreciation and higher rents in those areas. A good property locator would be aware of what's happening and know which properties fit the bill for investment.

The Property Manager

The final member of your PBI team, this individual is the buffer between you and the property. He or she is the person who finds the tenant and is responsible for rent collection. When the need for repairs arise, the property manager either makes them or contracts them out. A good property manager will not only find tenants and lease the property, but take phone calls from tenants even at night. Finding the right person for this position makes your investment experience a secure one instead of a constant worry.

As a lender, I have witnessed some of my investor clients accumulate property. The biggest indicator of their success was the fact that they quit their day jobs and started managing their own properties full time. You can do this if you'd like, but as you will see, it's not your only option.

You'll recall that my first PBI team included one of my mortgage clients who was a multiproperty owner/investor. It was easy for him to take on more properties to manage, so Ben and I came to a mutually beneficial agreement. Hiring him was much more attractive to me than trying to manage my own properties. He was very good at what he did—better than I would've been. And he had the time, while I didn't.

The key to hiring a property manager is doing what works best for you. For some investors, the thought of managing their own properties is appealing and adds security to their investment. If you have the time for this, by all means, go for it. But most, however, have day jobs and other responsibilities that keep them busy enough. They find the thought of having a knowledgeable, thorough, trustworthy expert watching over their investment for them to be far more attractive than trying to do it themselves. This is the route I chose. I'd rather push buttons.

> *"I started investing in 2003 with Ron's advice and now have four rental properties. His system has taken very little of my time to implement."*
>
> Andrew Hamilton
> *information services director*

More Complex Teams

Once you assemble a PBI team, you will feel much more confident about investing in real estate. Additionally, after you become the property owner, you will not feel nearly as anxious about your investments. You will have experts on your side—people as qualified or more qualified than you—doing the hard work.

I currently own several properties and have no hands-on responsibility. I sit at my desk, push buttons on my calculator, and enjoy investment success. I have effectively acquired real estate without the typical hassles of ownership by using a Push Button Investing team. (The last section of this book will instruct you in how to put one together for yourself.)

As we've said, the lender, locator, and property manager are the key players on a successful PBI team. There are, however, ways to further enhance your team and make it even more productive.

My holdings finally became so numerous that I decided I needed help pushing the buttons. So I went to my accountant for advice and was referred to Michele, also an accountant, who specializes in assisting businesses with their bookkeeping. Michele trained me to use a small business software program that would help me keep up with my real estate expenses and earnings. After a couple of sessions, I was able to display all of my property profit and loss statements on one screen. She then showed me how to e-mail the information to my Certified Public Accountant at year end to be reported on my taxes. I was so excited that I told some other investors. They hired Michele to teach them too. When your portfolio of properties grows large enough, I've found that a good accountant is also a great asset to your team.

Another person who would complement a PBI team is a rehabber. A rehabber is someone who can take a run-down or dated house and turn it into a desirable home. He or she can bring a home up to the current building code and provide new features that other older homes may not have. Sometimes the best areas for investment do not have an unlimited number of houses available for purchase. A rehabber can actually create product and accelerate appreciation. He or she can bring life to a whole street or neighborhood. A rehabber can also perform maintenance for your property manager at a lower cost than if you contracted it out.

An insurance agent may be another valuable member of a PBI team. Homes need to be insured. Yet successful PBI investors typically own several properties at a time, and some insurance companies limit the number of homes they will insure for an individual. When your real estate portfolio increases, it might therefore become beneficial to hire an agent who knows how to best insure multiple investment properties. The last thing you want to do is let insurance issues delay or abort purchases of profitable properties.

It is best that you start simple. Your PBI team can be extremely functional with the three original members I've described— lender, locator, and property manager—especially if you're not trying to own dozens of properties simultaneously. As my list of properties grew, I added professional members to enhance my efforts and further free up my time. Do this only if you feel it is helpful or necessary. Adding team members subsequently increased my team's ability to help other potential investors, like you, who heard of our success. Many of these people are now reaping great returns. I know you can, too.

PBI Notes

» The lender. Make sure that your lender knows investment financing and is working for your best interest.

» The property locator. Anyone can sell you a house. You want someone who can find homes with a high velocity of appreciation and in a good rental area.

» The property manager. Property management requires more than leasing your home and taking the tenant's phone calls. The manager must keep an eye on your investment.

» Go to my Web site at pushbuttoninvesting.com for information on active PBI teams.

PART TWO
GOALS AND OBJECTIVES

Investment Objectives

"You are about to experience a turning point. Stay in the game, it's too soon to quit!"

Van Crouch

Purchase with the Goal of Selling

I would consider my father, who has been in commercial real estate for over forty years, an expert in real estate investment. He always says, "You make your money when you sell."

In general, most real estate investors will either breakeven or produce a small cash flow during ownership. The big money is made when the property is sold. At that time, the investor will get his or her initial investment back—the down payment— plus a profit. If done properly, the profit will be many times the original investment. Multiply this profit by several properties and it's easy to understand how investors can quit their day jobs and invest in real estate full time. People who are buying their first home have a great opportunity to make money without tax consequences. During my twenty-plus-year lending career, most first-time home buyers have said they would be living in their new home for at least ten years, if not forever. It has been my experience, however, that first-time homeowners actually move in two to four years. They move due to job transfers, an increase in their family size, a boost in disposable income, or simply for a change of scenery. The point is that most first-time home buyers are unrealistic when it comes to the length of time they will stay in their homes.

Since most first-time home buyers will likely move by year four, they should plan accordingly. They should purchase their first home with the goal of selling. They should also purchase in an area of high appreciation.

I am a firm believer that your home is your shelter first and an investment second, but if you are now thinking of buying your first home, perhaps you can sacrifice lifestyle for a short time in order to reap a large return. Because statistics show that you will probably only be living there for a few years, it may be worth the extra $40,000 to $75,000 in equity that you can accumulate in a short period of time. In fact, you can profit from the sale of your primary home and be exempt from taxes on your gains. A single homeowner can sell their primary home, and subsequent primary homes, for accumulated gains of up to $250,000. A married couple is exempt from gains of up to $500,000. Consult your tax advisor for details. If you just want to "invest" your way to the house of your dreams, this is one way to do it. Furthermore, most freshman investors do not have the resources to start investing in real estate. If you initially make the right kind of purchase, your first home can actually fund your future real estate investments.

Holding Property for the Long Haul Is Not Necessary

The key to making income in real estate is the velocity of appreciation. This is the speed at which a property rises in value. Obviously, it is better to buy properties with a high velocity of appreciation. You want them to increase in value as fast as possible. By choosing properties with a high velocity of appreciation, you can profit faster—usually in five years. So it makes sense to invest only in properties of which this is true.

Monthly Rental Cash Flow Is Simply a Byproduct

As we have said, the big bucks are generated when a property is sold. Assuming the property purchase is based on the right information and has a high velocity of appreciation, your investment will be sound and you will benefit from investing.

Making money on a monthly basis is not necessary in the overall scheme, but it is important, especially when first starting out. It's helpful to be able to rent your investment property for enough to offset your monthly expenses (mortgage payment, maintenance, and property management costs). Your goal is to either break even or make a small profit while you hold the property. The investment objective is to not lose money during the holding process and then maximize your profits when the property is sold.

Lower Priced Properties Offer an Easy Entry Point

Sam, a mortgage client of mine, was eager to invest in real estate. He heard of people earning thousands of dollars, so he proceeded to set an appointment to meet with me. At our meeting, Sam presented a real estate flyer that described a home for sale. He thought the home was a great investment and wanted my opinion.

The home on the flyer was in a well-established area of town. The price was $350,000. Sam told me he wanted to make a 20 percent ($70,000) down payment. I looked at the flyer and asked Sam why he thought the home was a good investment. How was he going to make money on this home? Sam wasn't exactly sure.

In my opinion, even though the home was in a great area, it

was not a good investment. I told Sam that the amount of down payment that he was proposing would limit his present and future investing to this one home; he would not have additional funds to invest. Also, this home was not in a good rental area of town. The rents that he would need to cover his proposed monthly mortgage payment, plus expenses, would not be obtainable. He would sustain a loss each month that he owned the property.

Yet another reason why this home purchase did not make sense was that the area was not appreciating fast enough, and it would take too long to make a gain on the future sale. Finally, Sam would be relying on a renter whom he did not know to take care of this one-third of $1 million home. And since this would be his only investment, what if something happened to the house? Could he recover financially?

My advice to Sam was to buy lower priced properties. He could buy two homes for less than the home he was looking at. Additionally, he could buy in highly rentable areas that have a high velocity of appreciation. I referred Sam to a property locator who was building homes for investors. Sam ended up buying two homes for $150,000 each. His total investment for both houses was $30,000. His rents not only covered the monthly expenses but yielded over $300 per month profit per house. He was very happy that he sought out advice.

I understand that not everyone has $70,000 to invest. Sam was an exception. Yet in the end, he only spent a fraction of the money he had available. That's why buying a lower-priced home as an investment is attractive—the necessary cash upfront is less. Additionally, you are not exposed to as much risk involving property damage because the investment is not as substantial. Because Sam invested in a lower priced home, he was able to buy the initial two homes and two more a year later. Now he has four investment homes with money left over. Compare that to his original intention to invest all his money in one slowly appreciating home that would incur a monthly loss of income, and it is obvious why lower priced homes are usually the better investment.

PBI NOTES

» Purchase with the goal of selling. The day you sell is pay day.

» Holding property for the long haul is not necessary. Buy homes that appreciate quickly. Why wait a generation to be paid?

» Monthly cash flow is simply a byproduct. It is not necessary to make money while you own the property. As long as you break even during your holding period, you will be successful.

» Lower priced properties offer an easy entry point. Don't rely on a tenant to maintain an expensive property. You can buy more lower priced properties and spread your risk.

» To learn more about velocity of appreciation, go to my Web site at pushbuttoninvesting.com.

MAKE MONEY
WHEN YOU BUY

"You don't pay the price of success.
You enjoy the price of success."
Zig Ziglar

Receive Your Money When You Sell

Earlier, I quoted my father, who says, "You make your money when you sell." He is not entirely correct. Actually, you only receive your money when you sell. The money is made when you buy.

If you conduct proper research and locate a property with the potential for a high velocity of appreciation, you have already made your money. You physically receive that money after a brief holding period—typically four to five years—when you sell your property for a nice profit. Get into the habit of seeing the purchase of the property as the real money-making act. If you buy the right property, your money is already in the bank.

Locating Properties

Finding the right property is crucial for the PBI investor to be successful. Your locator must be able to find "pocket areas" that have high appreciation potential. This person must be able to see the future based on the area's characteristics and the history of similar markets. It should be noted that not all real estate agents are expert locators for PBI property, so you must be selective when choosing a property locator. This person must know the area backward and forward, its past and its potential. Let me give you an example of what I mean.

Two Identical Neighborhoods

I live in Dunwoody, Georgia, a suburb of Atlanta. The subdivision I live in is identical to the subdivision across the street. The houses are the same in size, style, age, and price range. The average person would not know there is a difference between the two neighborhoods. There is, however, a big difference.

Houses for sale in my subdivision stay on the market for about three weeks, while the adjacent subdivision's homes require up to three months to sell. It does not matter why this phenomenon exists. The important thing is to be aware of it. By knowing this information, an agent (or locator) would know how to price a home to sell it. Additionally, this person would know if there is room to negotiate on the price if representing a buyer. Ultimately, the buyer might pay close to the asking price on a house in my subdivision but would perhaps be able to pay less in the adjacent subdivision.

The point is simple: When finding a property locator for your investment home, it is important that the person you hire is aware of what is happening in the area in which you intend to buy. If you can buy a home at a lower price, or at a discount, you have already made money. Ideally, your locator will be an expert in areas that have a high velocity of appreciation.

Transitional Neighborhoods

There are many excellent properties in metropolitan areas that will achieve a high velocity of appreciation. Properties that are close-in tend to appreciate faster than properties in outlying areas. That's because properties in town and close to town offer a quicker commute to the central business district. There is usually public transportation available and a variety of cultural activities not found in outlying areas. The problem is that the well-established, in-town properties are very expensive and do not make economic sense for the PBI investor. There are, however, "pocket areas" that have a much lower price point. These are areas that have already transitioned, and they often make ideal push button investments.

Transitional neighborhoods are in-town pocket areas that have recently been or are being revitalized. The prices are still relatively low because people are at the beginning stage of moving back in. These areas offer the benefits of in-town living at a discounted price. They are close to major office buildings, public transportation, the arts, and myriad entertainment possibilities that only a city can support. It takes an expert locator to sniff them out.

A typical transitioning neighborhood might have some new construction, as well as existing homes that are being rehabilitated. Children are often seen at play in these neighborhoods, riding their bicycles in the streets. The strip malls nearby are filled with quality stores. These types of neighborhoods offer an excellent investment. By purchasing in a pocket area such as this, the PBI investor has made money up front and should make more as the home continues to appreciate at a rapid pace.

Get in on the Ground Floor

Have you ever noticed a subdivision or townhome community going up that seemed unique? Did you have a gut feeling that you should buy one of the homes because the community would sell out quickly? Was your assumption correct? Did the property sell out and were the prices higher afterwards? Did you figuratively kick yourself and say that you should have purchased? Now is the time to be aware of these opportunities as well.

You need to be able to envision unique projects. A developer may build a subdivision in town or build in a warehouse area that is in the center of the city. Become an expert and use the experience of your property locator. In-town properties usually have a higher velocity of appreciation.

If You Cannot Profit in a Short Period of Time, Do Not Buy

The savvy PBI investor knows that you should make your money when you buy. He or she also knows that any property purchased should have a high velocity of appreciation. If you can successfully purchase in-town or close-to-town investment property with this overarching characteristic, then it will not take long to achieve a nice profit. The quicker the property appreciates, the more successful you will become, and the sooner you will have more money to invest in other properties. Choose your investment properties carefully. Don't invest in areas that will appreciate slowly—there are other areas of town that can earn you money much quicker. Making the right choices upfront will take much of the worry and hassle out of investing.

Foreclosures

A client of mine named Evan buys foreclosures on the courthouse steps in a rural Georgia town. This town is approximately 45 miles away from metro Atlanta. Many residents commute from there to downtown Atlanta. The commute can take one to two hours, depending on traffic. Due to its proximity to downtown, this town is not a high appreciating area.

Evan purchases townhomes or single-family homes in foreclosure and makes cosmetic repairs, such as painting them and replacing carpet. After a minimum amount of this cosmetic work, the property may be worth $20,000 more. Yet in five years, the property may only increase in value by $5,000 to $10,000, so it does not make sense for Evan to hold and lease the property. If Evan has already made $20,000 within a month of the acquisition, he should sell and purchase his next investment with the profit. Foreclosures can be a good buy but not necessarily a good hold. Keep this in mind when pursuing this type of property. If it sits in an area where appreciation is slow, don't plan to hold onto it. Make some cosmetic improvements (if necessary) and then put it back on the market to realize your profit.

PBI NOTES

» You receive dollars when you sell. This is only if you buy the right property up front.

» Locating properties. Locating the right properties is crucial to your success.

» Two identical neighborhoods. Use an expert to help you find the right investment property. Don't use your mother's friend's daughter who just got her real estate license.

» Transitional neighborhoods. Urban areas that have become revitalized can be great investments.

» Get in on the ground floor. The beginning stages of large developments may prove to provide a rapid increase in value.

» Short-term profit. If you cannot profit in a short period of time, do not buy.

» Foreclosures. Recognize the market and act accordingly. Depending on the market, foreclosures may be better suited to sell quickly.

SUCCESSFUL
REAL ESTATE
INVESTING

"It's what you learn after you know it all that counts."

John Wooden

Most people feel that they should buy real estate. They know of others who have been successful, and they want a piece of the action. Yet I've found that many of these same investors delve into real estate on a whim or a gut feeling. At the least, many proceed without a proven plan. This is a recipe for disaster.

The Traditional Mindset

Craig is a client of mine who decided to become a real estate investor. He is a schoolteacher, coaches after school, and has an annual income of $45,000. Craig spent an entire weekend creating a real estate investment plan. He then made an appointment with me to talk about his future success.

When Craig arrived, he handed me a 10-page document and asked me to read it while he sat there. The document was his investment plan. The highlights of his plan were as follows. First, he would buy ten properties in a northern suburb of Atlanta for $100,000 each. The properties would be leased out for $1,000 per month. He would pay off the ten houses in ten years and then use the income as cash flow for his retirement.

As I read the plan, Craig appeared to get more and more excited. Unfortunately, his plan was typical of most first-time investors: there was no research supporting it. At best, the plan was wishful thinking on Craig's part. I struggled through his 10-page document and tried to help him make better decisions about his future in real estate investing.

There were major flaws in Craig's proposal. For one, the purchase price of $100,000 per property was unrealistic. A home in that area of town, in decent repair, would sell for at least $150,000. Secondly, there was no way to get rent close to $1,000 per month on a $100,000 home. Craig chose this area to invest in because it was "close by" and the properties would be convenient for him to manage. But what's the likelihood that he could manage the ten properties, work as a teacher and a coach, and then find time to spend with his wife and small children? Finally, the area of town Craig was considering was not appreciating quickly.

So how would Craig do it? The rents that he could realistically get would only allow him to break even after mortgage payments and expenses. Without a monthly cash flow, how would Craig pay off the mortgages on his ten houses in ten years? His teacher's salary is barely enough to cover his current expenses. The only way that he could pay off the ten mortgages is to get thirty-year mortgages that will be paid off after thirty years. And then there is the question of major repairs. Did he realize that he might have to replace the roof and the heating and air conditioning system twice over a thirty-year period? What about painting the outside and inside every five years? Of course, there would also be minor repairs, and perhaps the need to replace an appliance or two.

Clearly, Craig's numbers did not work. At most, he could own ten houses free and clear in thirty years. He would only break even along the way. Craig is 42 years old. If he could afford to buy ten houses at once and pay them off in thirty years, he could retire when he turned 72. Not a terrible plan, but not exactly desirable either. Yet this didn't matter because Craig could not afford to buy ten houses at once anyway; it would take him several years to do so. He might be lucky to retire on this plan when he reached 80.

Needless to say, I was not a big proponent of Craig's investment plan. It was, for all intents and purposes, doomed from the beginning. Unfortunately, many failures in real estate investing start the same way.

> *"Even though I've owned a rental home for many years, the information you presented provided me with new insight."*
>
> Darien Chimoff
> manager

Create a Perpetual, Annual Cash Flow

I believe there is a better way—Push Button Investing. It is simple and easy. It only requires purchasing one property a year in an area that has a high velocity of appreciation and a rental market that will cover the mortgage and monthly expenses of the investment home. Most of the properties that I buy with this strategy go up in value between $75,000-$100,000 over a five-year period.

Let's be conservative and assume that the properties increase by only $50,000 after a five-year holding period. The chart below shows that by purchasing one house a year, you can begin to realize a steady gain in your income after only five years. Imagine how much longer it would take to achieve this same pay increase in your current job.

YEAR	BUY	SELL	GAIN
1	2007		
2	2008		
3	2009		
4	2010		
5	2011		
6	2012	2007	$50,000
7	2013	2008	$50,000
8	2014	2009	$50,000
9	2015	2010	$50,000
10	2016	2011	$50,000

Here's an explanation of how our example works. You, the investor, buy a home the first year (2007) and lease it to cover your mortgage and expenses. A year later (2008), you buy another home and lease it out in the same manner. You continue this pattern for five consecutive years (through 2011). Then, in the sixth year (2012), besides buying a home, you also sell the first home you bought in 2007 for a gain of $50,000. In the seventh year (2013), you sell the second home you bought in 2008 for a gain of $50,000. This pattern—buying one home and selling another—continues every year from the fifth year on.

Within five years, this strategy creates an immediate, perpetual income. The real beauty of it is that you can be successful by owning only five houses at one time. Additionally, sticking with the plan only requires one home purchase per year. That gives you and your team 12 months to find an investment house to buy which has a high velocity of appreciation and is in a good rental area.

Unlike the traditional mindset, the PBI method hypothetically allows an investor to retire after only five years. As you can see, a perpetual, annual cash flow of $50,000 can easily be obtained. In fact, one could start investing at the age of 60 and still retire at 65. But imagine if the PBI investor begins at the age of 35. The possibilities are endless. He or she can generate income to live on by the time they are 40 years old. Or what if, instead of taking the gain each year, you reinvested it so you were buying two houses? In that case, you would be making $100,000 per year (the gain on two homes at $50,000 each) after 10 years.

The chart below, which begins in the sixth year of investment, in 2012, illustrates our second example:

YEAR	BUY	SELL	GAIN
6	2012 (2)	2007	Reinvest
7	2013 (2)	2008	Reinvest
8	2014 (2)	2009	Reinvest
9	2015 (2)	2010	Reinvest
10	2016 (2)	2011	Reinvest
11	2017 (2)	2012 (2)	$100,000
12	2018 (2)	2013 (2)	$100,000
13	2019 (2)	2014 (2)	$100,000
14	2020 (2)	2015 (2)	$100,000

*Once you start to sell your properties, you have the choice of reinvesting the gain or taking it out as income. Many of our PBI investors are doing both. By properly leveraging each investment, they are able to reinvest and have money left over to take out as income.

Another benefit to the PBI method is that because the holding time for each property is five years, the chances of incurring a major repair is slim. At the inspection of a new potential property, you can predict major repairs that may occur within the next five years. If there is the possibility of a major repair, you may choose to walk away from the deal and find another property, or perhaps negotiate a better purchase price.

Create Financial Freedom

Successful PBI investors have been able to create a predictable, annual income. It is as simple as it appears. This method of buying and selling is straightforward, and since the property is located and managed for you, you still have plenty of time to do what you want. Why wouldn't anyone want a $50,000-plus annual income with minimal effort?

I'll say it again. Most people want to invest in real estate, but most people do not know how to invest in real estate. By applying the principles of the PBI system, anyone can be successful. You can be successful without worry, hassle, or fear.

> *"Best financial move I have ever made!"*
>
> T. Darrell Albright
> sales manager

Push Button Investing Creates an Annuity

This book was written for the investor and the professional team members who help the Push Button Investor. The team members play a crucial role in the success of PBI. The locator must find properties that are easily leased and have a high velocity of appreciation. The manager must be able to find tenants, make or contract repairs, and take all calls related to the properties. The lender must be able to finance properties in such a way that it creates the lowest monthly payments for both experienced and inexperienced investors alike.

By following the PBI system, the team members can also create business they might otherwise not have. It has been my experience that the average homebuyer purchases a home every five years. Of course, the locater (typically a Realtor) and the lender earn a commission upon the closing of that sale (once every five years per client). PBI team members have the benefit of turning a once-every-five-years client into an annual home purchase client. Furthermore, your team members can create wealth for every client they encounter by introducing him or her to the PBI system. This becomes a win-win situation: The client makes an annual purchase / sale / gain, while the team member generates a commission on the purchase and sale each year. If a team member turns multiple clients into annuities, their income only increases and the benefits to their clients continue. If team members can create wealth for their clients, then their income is well-deserved.

PBI Notes

» Create a perpetual cash flow. Using the PBI system, you can build a predictable, annual income that can last for as long as you want it to.

» To stay current on investment strategies, go to my Web site at pushbuttoninvesting.com and sign up for my online newsletter.

CHANGE YOUR FINANCING MINDSET

"There is never any justification for things being complex when they could be simple."

Edward de Bono

Put 10 Percent Down

A prudent investor will acquire a rental home with a small cash investment. I recommend a 10 percent down payment. The rate on a mortgage is better with a 10 percent down payment versus a smaller down payment. Additionally, making a smaller down payment and financing a larger amount will only increase your monthly payments.

Aside from the percentage of the down payment and the size of the mortgage needed to acquire the property, there are other ways to lower your monthly payment. Let's take a look at them.

No Fixed Rates

The traditional 30-year fixed rate is the most common mortgage and the easiest to understand. It also has the highest interest rate that one can obtain. But remember, the PBI investor wants to have a payment that is as low as possible on an investment property. So the difference between a thirty-year fixed rate and a more suitable type of mortgage may mean a positive monthly cash flow on the property versus a monthly loss.

Hybrid Loans

The PBI model suggests that you hold onto a home for five years. A five-year waiting period will allow you to achieve the desired return upon the home's sale. (This assumes that the home is purchased correctly and has a high velocity of appreciation.) If the investment is held for just five years, then a thirty-year fixed rate is a waste of money. A hybrid mortgage is an adjustable rate mortgage (ARM) that has a fixed interest rate in the early years of the loan. Since the loan rate is adjustable after the fixed term of the mortgage, it generally offers a lower guaranteed start rate. A hybrid mortgage may have a fixed rate for one, three, five, seven, or ten years. The shorter the fixed period, the lower the initial interest rate. The mortgage that fits the PBI model the best is the five-year adjustable rate mortgage. Since it is adjustable at some point, the rate for the first five years is generally lower than on a thirty-year fixed rate mortgage. However, since you are selling your homes within five years of acquisition, the lower fixed rate on the hybrid mortgage will be long enough.

Interest-Only Loans

Another way to keep your monthly house payments down is to obtain an interest-only loan. Mortgage payments have traditionally been made up of both principal and interest. The principal portion of the payment allows the mortgage to be paid off in small amounts over a 30-year period. That small amount of principal paid against the mortgage is very little in the early years and increases over time.

If an investor holds a property for five years on a principal and interest mortgage, the mortgage is reduced very little upon the property's sale. An interest-only loan eliminates the principal portion of the payment and thus reduces the monthly payment on the home. This creates an even better cash flow for the investor. Interest-only loans are also available in one-, three-, five-, seven-, and ten-year adjustable rate mortgages. A PBI investor can usually obtain the lowest payment by obtaining a five-year adjustable rate mortgage that is interest-only.

Safe Mortgage Financing Options

30-Year Fixed   Highest Payment

Five-Year ARM   Lower Payment

Five-Year, Interest Only ARM   Lowest Payment

*You can obtain financing with much lower payments than the examples above. However, many of these options are considered unsafe because of deferred interest. Mortgages with deferred interest merely postpone the interest portion of the payment to drive down the payment. The interest that is postponed is added to the mortgage balance owed and is due in the future.

Examples of Mortgage Payments

Let's assume that you obtain a $150,000 mortgage to acquire your investment property. How much of a difference would there be in monthly payments using the three types of mortgages just outlined?

The five-year adjustable rate mortgage (ARM), with interest-only payments, has the lowest monthly obligation. By choosing this type of mortgage program, the PBI investor has a better opportunity to see a positive monthly cash flow. Below is an example of the monthly payments on a thirty-year fixed rate mortgage; a five-year ARM; and a five-year, interest-only ARM.

Thirty-Year Fixed at 6.25%	$923.58/month
Five-Year ARM at 5.5%	$851.68/month
Five-Year, Interest-Only ARM at 5.5%	$687.50/month

* Interest rates fluctuate perpetually. The interest rates quoted in these examples may not reflect the current market.

Obviously, in a real life situation where you are seeking to lease an investment home, the lower mortgage payments are more attractive. Let's assume that the home will lease for $1,400 per month and $250 per month is added to the mortgage payment for taxes and insurance. The example below shows the potential cash flow in each mortgage scenario.

Simple cash flow =

$1,400/month rent, minus $250/month for escrow, minus the mortgage payment

Thirty-Year Fixed
$1,400 − $250 − $923.58 = **$226.42 cash flow**

Five-Year ARM
$1,400 − $250 − $851.68 = **$298.32 cash flow**

Five-Year, Interest-Only ARM
$1,400 − $250 − $687.50 = **$462.50 cash flow**

You can see that the five-year, interest-only ARM offers a far better cash flow. The $462.50 per month gives the investor more flexibility. The extra money can be saved for future repairs, used to prepay the mortgage at a faster pace, or might even allow the investor to offset a negative cash flow on other properties. Additionally, if the rents in the area are lower, the use of the five-year interest-only ARM may mean the difference between just breaking even and enjoying a cash flow. The bottom line is that by choosing this option, the PBI investor can take advantage of more opportunities.

PBI NOTES

» The Push Button Investing method suggests that you own a property for five years with the lowest possible monthly cost.

» The safest mortgage financing option needed to accomplish this is a five-year, interest-only adjustable rate mortgage.

PART THREE
REAL ESTATE CHARACTERISTICS

LOCATION, LOCATION, LOCATION! WHAT DOES IT MEAN?

"There is a way to do it better—find it!

Thomas Edison

Location is the golden rule in real estate. It is the first lesson learned in just about every book, class, and seminar on selling or acquiring property. The idea is that the better the location, the more valuable the home, and therefore, the better the investment. The biggest question is: What is the best location? So many investors make bad location decisions, and hence, bad investments. Our goal is to avoid this fate.

Leasing Properties Nearby Is Not Important

I regularly meet with clients who want to buy investment properties in bad locations. This classic mistake can be illustrated by the story of Beth, a successful executive who lives in the suburbs away from town.

Beth makes a good salary and has extra cash, so she decided to become a real estate investor. She knew it would be a wise move. Yet she made the same assumption most beginners make.

Beth was determined to buy a rental close to her home in the suburbs so that she could self-manage the property. She knew enough to be dangerous. But what Beth did not know is that convenience is not important when buying investment property. The most important factor is the location, which may not be close to home.

In general, suburban communities offer a low velocity of appreciation and do not have a high concentration of renters. Investing in these outer areas of town is generally a bad idea in terms of both appreciation and rent.

On the other hand, properties closer in and around town have a high velocity of appreciation. They also have a larger population of renters. If Beth had embraced the PBI system, she would have hired a team that could locate and manage a faster-appreciating property.

Buy in the Hot Section of Town

The basic objective in business is to buy low and sell high. It does not matter that the investment property is located somewhere that is inconvenient to the investor. As long as the investment has a high velocity of appreciation and can be managed by an experienced PBI manager, the investment will be profitable.

Beth ended up with an average investment. She personally managed a property close to her suburban home and did not reap the returns she had hoped for. In many cases, people invest in real estate without the guidance or direction of a professional. In some cases, these "do-it-yourself" investors who are happy, successful executives may transform into frustrated investors who take their problems to the workplace.

Buy on the Water

Properties on lakes, rivers, and the coast also have a high velocity of appreciation. Waterfront properties are finite. As they are bought up, they become more and more scarce. That scarcity of supply creates greater demand. The greater the demand, the higher the price. If a PBI investor wants a waterfront property, he or she should purchase now, because as time goes by, the value of the property will increase.

Out-of-State Network

The PBI investor is always looking to profit from fast-appreciating properties. Since the location of the investment property does not need to be convenient to home, a qualified PBI team can handle the property no matter where it is located—even if it is out-of-state.

Property locators, if they are Realtors, usually network with other Realtors nationwide. They are likely to attend national conventions and seminars where they meet and exchange information with others in their field. This is great for you, the investor.

> *"I live in Georgia, but bought property in Texas. With Ron's system, you do not have to be in the same city or even the same state as your investment property."*
>
> Andrew Hamilton
> information services director

Your PBI team may have contacts who can provide you with other investment opportunities outside the area in which you live. This means that if there aren't any good real estate investments in your city, your team's network might place you with another PBI team. Again, there are no limitations to where you might invest. As long as there are properties with a high velocity of appreciation and effective PBI teams to utilize, you have an unlimited source of quality investments.

PBI NOTES

» Location. Buy in areas that have a high velocity of appreciation.

» Leasing properties close by is not important. The important thing is to buy properties that will make you money no matter where they are located.

» Buy in the hot section of town. Wouldn't you prefer to buy in an area where values are rising?

» Buy on the water; this type of land is limited. Demand for waterfront properties is increasing.

» Out-of-State. You are investing to profit. If property values are increasing in other states, you can still take advantage of that opportunity.

» To view a list of Push Button Investing teams, please visit my Web site at: pushbuttoninvesting.com.

WARNING!
YOU ARE NOT
MOVING IN

*"Procrastination is opportunity's
natural assassin."*

Victor Kram

Story of a Suburban Realtor

Diane is a residential real estate agent. She lives, works, and sells property in an expensive suburb of town. She is used to large, two-story homes with custom kitchens on large, wooded lots. It is not unusual for the properties she sells to have separate media rooms and an in-ground pool with manicured landscaping. Diane was familiar with my success in real estate investing and wanted to become an investor herself. We spent a long time talking about my homes. I explained how I would only buy in areas that had a high velocity of appreciation. My objective, I explained, was to buy, make a handsome gain in five years, and then sell. She decided to take the plunge and invest in something herself.

First, we spoke about hiring a manager to oversee the property. Next, I had my property locator provide a few excellent home listings that would fit the PBI model. Diane went out to view the properties and spent a lot of time looking, but she did not buy. A few weeks passed and I called Diane about some other excellent properties that had become available. Again, she spent time looking but did not buy. On each occasion, the properties were priced right, were highly rentable, and were located in an area with a proven high velocity of appreciation. Yet in the end, Diane was simply afraid to buy.

You Do Not Need the Amenities That You Are Used To

One of Diane's issues was that she could not separate her lifestyle from the investment properties. She could not see herself living in these homes, and therefore concluded that she could not buy them.

One of the most difficult concepts for a successful investor is buying beneath their means. The type of property that fits this description is unfamiliar, and as a result, often undesirable and intimidating. However, in order to be successful, you need to separate your life from your investments. I explained this to Diane and she agreed with me, but she still was afraid of the unknown. I shared with her that it takes courage to be successful. She thought about it and realized I was right. She bought one house and then another. Both were great buys, and they quickly rented for a positive cash flow. Through the encouragement of a PBI team and a change of mindset, she is now a successful PBI investor.

Serving a Purpose

Investing in residential real estate helps provide functional, safe homes for people. You are providing shelter for families. Most families do not need an elaborate suburban home. They need a clean, safe house that you and your PBI team can offer.

Typically, there is a lot of rental housing available in pocket areas. The problem is, not much of it is good quality. By utilizing an experienced PBI team, you can obtain quality homes that are highly rentable because they stand out amidst the many other lower quality choices. At the same time, you will be providing a great service to people who may otherwise not be able to afford a nice, in-town home.

PBI NOTES

» You need to put your real estate investment in perspective. You are not moving in, you do not need a whirlpool bath, and you do not need a swim and tennis facility. You are providing a quality home for a family who may not have the ability to buy one.

Properties That Would Appreciate

"Why not go out on a limb?
Isn't that where the fruit is?"

Frank Scully

Single-Family Homes

A low-priced, single-family home is the bread and butter of residential real estate investing. These homes may be acquired with a small down payment and leased with little effort. Additionally, mortgage financing is plentiful. A successful investor can own several of these small homes versus one or two large ones. The single-family rental home should be the anchor in your real estate portfolio.

I have worked with very successful investors who only own single-family homes. If you are successful with this type of investment, there is no need to change your strategy. From time to time, there may be opportunities to invest in other types of properties. Although buying different properties may be profitable, they should be acquired with caution and reserved for the more experienced investor. I have listed some of these other real estate opportunities in this chapter.

Vacation Homes

Demographics are giving us an important message. The largest generation of our country's citizens—the baby boomers—are beginning to retire. As they retire, many will downsize and buy a home in a vacation setting. Since we are at the beginning stages of this massive shift, now is the best time to buy. Supply cannot keep up with demand, and property values will undoubtedly rise. So buy a vacation home before prices increase.

If you are not in a position to afford another mortgage and enjoy the home yourself, then perhaps you could rent it out to supplement the payments. In many parts of the country, vacation homes have doubled in price in a very short period of time. While they don't fit the typical PBI model, such properties, if you are in a position to afford them, can serve as a great long- or short-term investment.

Lots in Vacation Areas

Many investors understand the appreciation they can achieve by buying a vacation home. However, mountain homes and lake homes may be in remote areas where a manager for the property is unavailable, and some investors just do not want the responsibility of renting a property that is not close by. Yet these investors can still achieve the benefits of property appreciation by purchasing a lot in a vacation area.

There are many benefits to owning a lot. The cost of a lot is a fraction of the price of a home, making it feasible for you to use some of your positive cash flow from other properties to pay the mortgage. Additionally, there is no upkeep or maintenance required on a raw piece of land. And the loan needed to acquire a lot is significantly less than for a house. Appreciation will still be achieved. The land is what becomes scarce, and when this happens, it will appreciate. The profit you can make on such a lot is substantial.

Condominiums in Densely Populated Areas

Close-in land in most major cities is very expensive and the cost is prohibitive. That's why condominiums are the answer to housing for in-town living. Condos offer many housing units on one piece of land. This allows home ownership for people who otherwise would have to pay a fortune for in-town living. The key to success with condominium investing is to buy close-in where there are few new condominium projects under construction. If there is no significant amount of available housing, the velocity of appreciation will be high.

Identifying Markets

We've already discussed why a "pocket area" in town is one of the best places to buy real estate for investment. This area has risen from the ashes and is typically a transitional neighborhood. It may take a lot of driving and research to find one of these pockets, but once you do, you will have a large supply of potentially great investment homes.

> *"Ron helped me understand that the best deals are often in areas that are being rediscovered and improved."*
>
> Andrew Hamilton
> information services director

In pocket areas, there are opportunities to buy homes that are ready to rent, as well as those that need refurbishing. If you have a rehabber on your PBI team, you can create homes for investment. A home to be rehabbed is bought at a lower price and the appreciation is already built in. After a five-year holding period, your investment is worth significantly more.

People all over the country double their money in a year when they invest in pocket areas. Sometimes this fantastic return is achieved by mistake. And although there is nothing wrong with that, wouldn't it be better to see a predictable return? If you can identify these pockets ahead of time, you will be ready to profit. Do your homework, or have someone on your team do it for you, as it will surely pay off.

PBI Notes

» Low-priced, single-family homes. A single-family home is the most common form of residential ownership. It is also the easiest to finance.

» Vacation homes. As demand increases, supply will diminish. Buy before prices rise.

» Lots in vacation areas. This is a less expensive way to invest in developing areas.

» Condominiums in densely populated areas. Condominiums can be a lucrative investment where housing demand is high and land is expensive.

» Identifying markets. Keep your eyes open. There are opportunities all around you. In order for you to be successful, the property should have a high velocity of appreciation and be in a good rental market.

» Go to my Web site at pushbuttoninvesting.com for information on vacation homes.

Real Estate That May Not Appreciate

*"Even if you're on the right track,
you'll get run over if you just sit there."*

Will Rogers

Investing in real estate, stocks, bonds, or even gold may be very lucrative. People have earned a lot of money investing in the right thing at the right time. On the other hand, people have lost a lot of money with the wrong investments. In real estate, it is important to either be an expert yourself or rely on an expert to ensure that you are buying the right properties. That said, there is some real estate in you should usually avoid investing in.

Condominiums in Less Dense Areas

Condominiums were created to offer home ownership on land that is jointly owned by the homeowners. Condos thrive in areas where land is too expensive for single-family homes. Instead of spreading out the community horizontally over many acres of land, condos are built vertically, and one condo project can offer home ownership to many on a small piece of real estate. This makes economic sense. However, when condominiums are built in less expensive, rural areas, they defeat the original purpose of a condo. In rural areas, land is cheap and it makes more sense to build horizontally.

Successful investing requires some amount of common sense. Condominiums in areas where land is relatively cheap do not have a high velocity of appreciation. As an investor, you should avoid such properties even though the lower price may be appealing.

Real Estate Investment Trusts (REITs)

A Real Estate Investment Trust (REIT) is a portfolio of real estate in which an investor can own a small share. Run in a manner similar to a mutual fund, an investor buys shares and a REIT manager is in charge of investing the money in profitable properties. This allows a small investor to buy real estate without having to locate or manage the property. A REIT may invest in office buildings, shopping malls, apartment complexes, parking lots, or even strip malls. Some buy only one type of property and others buy a mixture. Like mutual funds, there are REITs that make money and those that do not.

Because a REIT is a large entity, it may not allow the type of returns that a PBI investor can obtain. The REIT manager has to invest continually; there cannot be millions of dollars sitting idle in the trust. That means the timing may not be right to buy the best properties, and the result can be poor or unnecessarily risky investments.

Since a REIT is a very large investor, each investment made must be large. Because it would be too cumbersome for the REIT to buy single-family homes, investors miss some of the best returns in real estate. Furthermore, a REIT cannot work efficiently in pocket areas of town. It may obtain a small return here and there, but PBI investors who buy residential real estate can consistently make more money per dollar invested.

Peak-Priced Properties

Many investors buy the right properties at the wrong time. The PBI investor should avoid buying peak-priced properties. In 2003-2005, people flocked to coastal areas and bought condos and single-family homes. Many of these homes appreciated 50 percent to 100 percent over this short period of time.

I was in south Florida visiting relatives and I witnessed this buying frenzy firsthand. People I knew bought and sold properties and made hundreds of thousands of dollars. In one case, an investor contracted to build a home for $750,000 and sold that same home for $1.2 million before completion. Many of these people were driving expensive cars for the first time in their lives. They were only buying and selling a few houses a year. It was like shooting fish in a barrel, and there was no end in sight.

I looked at this incredible, short-term appreciation and started to wonder when it would stop. The huge appreciation was occurring because the supply of homes could not keep up with the demand. Then I looked around and it hit me. I saw, in a nutshell, what was going to happen. There were high-rise condominiums coming out of the ground in every direction that I looked. Once this new supply of homes would hit the market, it would grossly outnumber the demand. Simple economics tell us that when supply is greater than demand, prices will fall. For the time being, prices in Florida are still at their peak. Do not invest at peak prices. Eventually, they will fall, once the supply catches up.

Much of this coastal buying was generated by investors. It is not reasonable to think that there are enough owner-occupants and vacation homeonwers (end users) to afford to buy a steady stream of $1–$3 million homes. The prices of these homes were driven up by investors. Once the end users stop buying, the market for these homes will soften. When this happens prices will fall.

PBI Notes

» Velocity of appreciation. It is important to choose properties that appreciate quickly.

» Condominiums. Avoid buying condos in areas of town where land is less expensive.

» REITs. By investing in a REIT, you own a small portion of the investment, similar to owning shares of a mutual fund. You have no control of the management of your investment.

» Peaked-priced properties. Common sense tells you to buy low and sell high. Start to recognize the characteristics of areas in which you may want to invest.

12
BUILDING A REAL ESTATE PORTFOLIO

*"If you can dream it,
you can do it ..."*
Walt Disney

Many of us have a 401(k) or a brokerage account that includes
a variety of stocks. Investing in company stock is common, but
the returns can be unpredictable. We discussed earlier how the
stocks of many financially solid corporations dropped in value
overnight due to a product recall or a scandal with one of their
principals. If, however, you spread your stock investments among
different industries and sizes of companies, your portfolio is
more balanced and you reduce your risk. Financial advisors will
tell you that it is generally wise to own many stocks, so that on
average, the value overall of your overall holdings will increase.

This classic investment strategy has proven to be successful for decades. The same strategy holds true for real estate. You can build an investment portfolio that is safe due to its diversity yet still follows your PBI strategy.

Most of us own a primary home, which may be our first and biggest real estate investment. Your primary home can also become the first holding in your real estate portfolio. By building a portfolio, you can diversify your real estate investments, much like a stock portfolio. This will reduce your risk and put you in a much better position to profit. Here are some suggestions on how you can diversify.

Rental Homes in Other Parts of Town

It is common for real estate investors to acquire properties in the same general area. But after acquiring a few investment homes, you should consider buying in another part of town. Doing so will help you are diversify your investments. If something happens in an area that may affect one of your investments, you will still have homes in other parts of town that will not be affected. If you follow the PBI system, you can buy property in any part of town because the management is handled for you.

Vacation Properties

In the past, I was not a proponent of purchasing vacation properties. My philosophy was that by the time you paid the mortgage and upkeep on a vacation home, the annual cost would far exceed the charges for staying at a five-star hotel for a month. Additionally, I thought you would be stuck going to your vacation home all the time instead of choosing any number of other locations to visit. Recently, I changed my mind.

I was a guest of a friend at his lake home. We enjoyed skiing and wakeboarding all day. I was intrigued by the homes on the lake. I asked about the price of the homes and was shocked. My friend told me that if I could find a lot, the price would range from $750,000 to $800,000. He also said that five years ago, the price for the very same lots was $150,000 to $200,000, which was considered a high price at that time. Once I returned home, I did some research of my own and confirmed the prices that my friend had given me. I looked at other lake properties and saw the same pattern of appreciation. This looked like a great investment. But to make sure, I did more research.

The results of my research helped me conclude that investing in lakefront property is usually a good investment if you can get in at the right time. I found article after article that discussed vacation homes. The consistent message was that over the next ten to fifteen years, the baby boomers would be retiring. The boomer population is the large group of Americans born in the eighteen-year period (1946-1964) following World War II. The majority of the people in this generation follow similar behavior patterns, including the way they purchase real estate.

Baby boomers bought their first homes in the 1970s and 1980s. Many of them upgraded to a nicer home five to ten years later. Now, baby boomers are getting ready to retire. This will result in yet another shift in their real estate needs and their buying habits.

According to the April 11, 2005 edition of BusinessWeek, "boomers, in particular, are driving the second home market with an eye toward both investment and future retirement."[6] It is expected that they will be downsizing their homes and purchasing smaller retirement and vacation type properties. For investors, that means now is the time to invest in these types of homes.

There are several types of properties suitable for investment, the most popular being lakefront homes, mountain homes, and beach homes. A shrewd investor might buy a second home in a vacation or resort area ahead of the influx of retiring boomers. Another reason that people—not just boomers—purchase second homes is to be close to a family member or a frequently visited business destination.

If you are an investor, it is important to understand that a vacation home serves a dual purpose. The primary purpose should be that of enjoyment for you and your family. Whether it is skiing, hiking, or lounging on the beach, a family that plays together, stays together.

The second purpose for a vacation home is for investment. The right property bought at the right time should provide a handsome profit when sold. Or, if you plan to keep the vacation home for a longer period of time, you can also use the equity the home accumulates to invest in other properties.

In order to capitalize on the best return from a vacation home, you must be flexible. Not too long ago home prices on the Florida coast took a major spike upward and were considered to be overpriced. An alternative to a Florida property might have been a gulf front beach property in Alabama. The sand and the sun are the same but the price may have been substantially cheaper. Additionally, the travel time to an Alabama beach may be less.

The same holds true for lakefront property. A flexible real estate investor can find lower priced lots by going to a lesser-known lake. It is important to note that in order to buy a second home, it must be affordable. Buying at a lower price point in a lesser-known area is not only more affordable, it also leaves room for further investments.

If you are a really flexible, courageous investor, you should buy what is not hot. Over the past five years, there has been a run-up on Florida beach homes and condominiums. Therefore, Florida beach properties are very popular (hot) and homes are listed at peak prices. At the same time, mountain properties have not been as popular. With lower prices, these homes have remained inexpensive. Buying a mountain home now would allow you to buy at the low end of the price range.

Another way to purchase a vacation home in the lower price range is to buy in the off-season. In winter, many lakes are partially drained because they are regulated by power companies. The demand for lakefront properties is lower during this time because the cold weather and the poor appearance of the lake keeps buyers away.

Many people vacation in the mountains in the summer due to the cooler climate. Demand for these homes is also lower in the winter months due to inclement weather. Many builders who have mountain homes for sale might offer them at lower prices during the slow winter months in order to move inventory. Keep your eyes open for such opportunities.

The proximity of your vacation home is also crucial. It should be no more than a two- to three-hour drive from your primary residence. This will allow you to enjoy the home many times a year. If it is more than a short drive away, it is likely that you will not use it very often. It would then shift from a vacation home to an expensive rental home. A second home is not for everyone; make sure you are going to use it before you buy.

Building Lots

A lot, suitable for building on in the future, is an inexpensive way to acquire real estate. The price is usually about 25 percent of the cost of a home. Lots can be bought and owned without the need for a property manager. They offer an easy entry price for those who do not want to make a higher investment and are not interested in the upkeep of a house. Yet lots also will create a profit if bought in the right area.

My friend, Alex, built a home on a lake and purchased the lot next door. He enjoyed spending time at his lakefront home with his family and had no intention of selling. About ten years later, his children were entering college and the tuition was starting to take a toll on Alex's finances.

I was having coffee with Alex one morning, and he explained how he wanted to hold on to his lake house, but the mortgage payments had become a burden amidst the added college tuition expenses. I asked him if he still owned the adjoining lot. He said he did, but he did not realize it was worth substantially more after ten years.

As it turned out, Alex ended up selling the lot. The proceeds from the sale netted more than enough to pay off the mortgage on his lakefront house. Thus, Alex was able to eliminate this payment and, more importantly, hold on to the lake home that he and his family loved.

Alex originally bought the lot because it was so cheap. He did not need it, but nevertheless was able make a huge profit in a relatively short period of time. The right land purchased at the right price is an easy, no-maintenance way for the PBI investor to earn money.

PBI Notes

» Building a real estate portfolio allows you to diversify your risk.

» Rental homes in other parts of town. You can diversify just by varying the locations of your investments.

» Vacation properties. Demand is starting to pick up for leisurely living. Buy before prices rise.

» Building lots. Acquiring land without a home on it allows you to purchase appreciating property without the need for management.

» Go to my Web site at pushbuttoninvesting.com to view my sample online real estate holdings statement.

Thinking Outside the Box

"The greatest mistake a man can make
is to be afraid of making one."

Elbert Hubbard

There are many people making money in real estate in many different ways. We hear stories about how a small fortune was made in an unusual manner. Yet in many cases, the people were lucky. They happened to buy in the right place at the right time. Others have made money through the sale of property that was acquired through inheritance. They did no footwork to actually earn the money; it was a gift.

It would be great to be handed an asset that was held for many years and is now worth a fortune, but most of us do not have this coming, and the odds are very good we will not succeed through luck. The PBI system set forth in this book allows the average person—like you and me—to succeed in real estate investing. We don't have to be lucky and don't need a lot of money to get started. Best of all, there are more investment options than most of us realize. Here are a few more that I haven't yet mentioned.

Kiddie Condos

A kiddie condo is a term used to describe a condominium that a parent has purchased for a child to live in while attending college. Because the student was going to be living in the college town for at least four years, the logic was obvious: Why not own the home my child lives in versus renting for the duration? This concept has caught on and has become very popular. Although it is called a kiddie "condo," the property might also be a single-family home.

There are definite advantages to buying a condo or a single-family home for your college student. The interest paid on the house each year is tax deductible. In addition, since the student is occupying the property, the best mortgage financing options and terms may be available. Owner occupied properties carry a lower interest rate than mortgages on investment properties. Furthermore, your child's roommates can become renters for the other rooms, which may provide enough income to cover the mortgage payment. Your child ends up living for free in a home you own but don't pay for. The best part is that at the end of four years, you typically can sell the home for a profit. For four years you spend nothing on your child's rent, your mortgage is paid for, and you make money in the process. Not a bad deal.

Still, like any other property, kiddie condos or single-family homes for kids should be chosen with caution. The PBI system suggests that you buy in areas that have a high velocity of appreciation. And with college towns, determining appreciation can be tricky.

Major cities where colleges are located will have a variety of housing options. Often, there are pocket areas in these cities that meet the PBI system's higher appreciation requirements. It may, however, be more difficult to find good investments when the college is in a smaller town.

These small "college towns," as we typically call them, generally exist because of the economics of a major university. Without the university, the town would barely survive. Appreciation in real estate generally occurs when there is a shift or influx of population: the greater the demand for housing, the greater the appreciation. Unfortunately, most small college towns do not experience a big increase in population. College enrollment itself does not grow enough to cause rapid appreciation. Therefore, in smaller towns, it is all the more important to carefully consider the location before buying property. If it looks as though a high velocity of appreciation is questionable, it's still okay to buy if your child can live there for free during his or her college years and your mortgage will be paid. But the ideal scenario is one where the home also appreciates over your four years of ownership. This way, you will do more than simply recoup your original investment—you will also make good money in the process.

John and his wife wanted to invest in real estate. Unfortunately, they could not do so because of the huge expenses they were paying to send their son to college. Their son attended college in another state. Not only did they have to pay the higher "out-of-state" tuition, but room and board was increasing as well. John came to me wanting to refinance his primary home and lower his monthly payments in order to get some relief from his large, college related expenses. However, a refinance would not save John much money. In order to help John out, I asked him a few questions about the housing near the college. As it turned out, the college was in an area of high student housing demand. I suggested that John buy a home near the college so that his child could live there rent-free. John could rent out the rooms and the monthly rent would pay the mortgage.

John thought about it and decided to move forward. He started looking at homes to buy. Finally, he narrowed his search down to two homes—a three bedroom and a four bedroom. In addition to having an extra bedroom, the four bedroom home had more living space. It was only $10,000 more in price. John felt that the lower priced home would better fit his budget, but I convinced him to buy the bigger home. As a result, the extra rent from the fourth bedroom more than offset the extra cost of the home. John was now very happy. He was able to send his son to college and avoid paying for housing. He could write off the mortgage interest on his taxes. Best of all, he bought himself a property that is in a very tight housing market, which will make him a nice profit when he sells.

But the story does not stop there. In order to get the best mortgage pricing, John added his son, the owner-occupant, to the title. Since his son was now a property owner in that state, his tuition changed to "in- state" status and it dropped by $14,000 per year. The purchase became a windfall for John. His cash flow improved because his son's housing was covered by the rent, he saved a huge amount annually by avoiding "out-of-state" tuition, he gained favorable tax treatment, and he had the real estate investment that he thought he could not afford.

Executive Rentals

The PBI system suggests that an investor buy moderately priced properties. By doing so, there is less upkeep, and the lower rent offers housing for a greater percentage of the population. There are, however, situations where higher priced homes may be acquired for a bargain.

At the time this book was written, the U.S. Federal Reserve was systematically raising short-term interest rates. Not long before that, the craze was to sell people more mortgage than they could afford. One-month and six-month interest-only adjustable rate mortgages allowed people to buy high-priced properties with incredibly low payments. Interest rates were in the high 2 percent range. A $600,000 mortgage cost $1,375 a month and a $1 million mortgage cost about $2,300 a month. People seized this opportunity and bought homes they normally could not afford.

Today, the ongoing rates on these mortgages are significantly higher than their low introductory offers. As a result, many people's payments have more than doubled. Unfortunately, short-term rates are still rising. More and more people who overextended themselves are now experiencing payment shock. Many of these people will need to sell quickly in order to get out of the higher mortgage obligation. Some may lose their homes in foreclosure. This type of situation creates an opportunity for the PBI investor.

Perhaps you're in a position to buy a home at a $100,000-$200,000 discount? You can then hold the property for a year or so and pocket a large profit. Of course, the key to this strategy is covering your payments while owning the property—something that is typically difficult to do in a higher-priced home. The type of renter you are looking for is going to be unique. The renter must be able to afford higher payments but have no interest in ownership. Believe it or not, there is such a person: the executive renter.

Companies headquartered in other cities often relocate their executives on a temporary basis to different regions of the country. If an executive owns a home in New York and is on temporary assignment in Atlanta, he usually keeps his New York home and rents a temporary executive-type home in Atlanta. This is an ideal scenario for the investor. By renting to executives like the New Yorker, you can acquire and hold a more expensive property. And believe it or not, this can happen in any city. It allows you, the PBI investor, to buy a higher priced home at a discount and realize a nice profit within one or two years.

Executive rental homes do not have to be million dollar properties. Depending on the region of the country, this executive rental strategy can be profitable using homes in the $250,000 to $500,000 price range. Additionally, executive renters do not need to be business executives. Nancy, a locator in Atlanta, specializes in the mid- to high-$200,000 price range. She leases her homes to a variety of professional, medical, and university people. The homes that Nancy specializes in are near Emory University.

When I first met Nancy, I asked her about leasing to people who could afford the high rents of luxury apartments. Why would they move into a house when they can get all the amenities of an entire upscale apartment community? Nancy gave me many reasons. She explained that often people have pets, so they need a yard for their dog. Many people have children and want to raise their kids in an environment that is more conducive to family life. Finally, she pointed out that you cannot beat the peace and quiet of a home.

Nancy's explanation made sense. For the first time, I conceded that there might be a medium price rental market for the Push Button Investor. But to make sure, I asked her, "Who's going to lease these properties and how are you going to locate these people?"

Nancy was very confident in her answer. The sources of renters that she named seemed so obvious. She could easily and regularly obtain quality tenants who would need two- and three-year leases. The university area was a prime source for students and professors with multiyear rental needs: medical students, physicians in fellowship programs, graduate students, theology students, law students, nursing school students, visiting professors, and Center for Disease Control employees. Clearly, Nancy had a good thing going, and her success provides a great example of what you can accomplish by purchasing executive rentals.

Keep in mind, however, that PBI is based on fast property appreciation. While there may be executive renters in droves near a university, the properties themselves may not appreciate much, if any, over the course of a few years. This is especially true—as we've already said—when the university is in a smaller town. While you need not shy away from such opportunities if the price is a great bargain, this type of investing should be reserved for experienced investors.

Be especially careful when purchasing executive type homes. Your locator should do his or her homework to ensure that a large business or university is nearby and will keep the demand up for executive rental properties. (One source that may enable your property manager to advertise executive properties for lease is craigslist.com. Craig's List reports, among other things, properties for lease in almost every city in the country. In many metropolitan areas, the Realtors' Multiple Listing Service also offers executive rental listings which you can utilize.)

Take note that executive rentals entail more risk because the acquisition cost is greater and the income required monthly to cover your larger mortgage payments and other expenses is higher. If you are new to real estate investing, I recommend that you buy lower-priced properties to gain experience and momentum. As you succeed, executive rentals might then offer you a way to diversify your real estate portfolio and enhance your profitability.

Fastest-Growing Towns

You never know where you might learn lessons on investing. It may even be on a cruise ship. I was recently on a cruise with my family, and we were out at sea for a day while traveling to our next port. For those of you unfamiliar with cruising, the ship provides activities for guests while they are at sea. My wife and I chose to participate in a "Rock and Roll" trivia contest to pass the time.

The leader of the contest put us into groups so that the contest would be more manageable. We joined forces with a mom and her daughter. Between questions, we socialized and learned about each other. The mom had been divorced for about two years. She described how it was initially very difficult to begin a new life as a single mom. She had no savings or assets to speak of. She had to downsize her home. Fortunately, she did some research during that hard time and decided to buy a smaller home in a nearby town—a town considered to be one of America's fastest growing. Within one year of ownership, her $170,000 home was worth $270,000. She was able to increase her wealth by $100,000 in one year.

This type of growth is happening all over the country. It takes some research to determine exactly where, but there are always opportunities. The PBI investor knows that any town where phenomenal growth is occurring should be investigated. Remember, you do not have to move into the property; it is a rental home. Therefore, it does not matter where the property is located, because you can rely on a local PBI team to take care of your investment.

Through traveling, I have learned a tremendous amount about

people and their investments. This single mom reminded me of an important investing lesson: Growth is always occurring somewhere, and there may be great opportunities associated with it. We just have to look for that growth and then determine how we can capitalize on it.

PBI Notes

» There are many ways to make money using the PBI system.

» Kiddie condos. Take advantage of having children. Many people have actually made money while their kids were in college.

» Executive rentals. There are many fast appreciating properties that are higher priced.

» Fastest growing towns. There are always some areas experiencing exceptional growth. Take advantage of them.

PART FOUR
MANAGING YOUR PROPERTIES

HAVE YOUR CAKE
AND EAT IT, TOO

*"The successful person is the one who
went ahead and did the thing
I always intended to do."*

Ruth Smeltzer

You are considered to be successful at Push Button Investing when you hold property, cover the mortgage with rental income, and then sell the property for a handsome gain. Making money while the property is held is not the primary objective. But what if you could make a sizable profit while holding the property? Here's how it can be done.

Government Housing Assistance Programs

Most major cities in the United States offer government assisted

145

rental programs. The most commonly known program is called Section 8. It is designed to provide free or subsidized rent vouchers to families in need of quality housing. Investors who offer their homes to Section 8 tenants receive electronic rent payments directly from the government on the first of every month.

Your property needs to be in good condition if you want to participate. Below are a few of the minimum standards your property must meet when participating in a government assisted rent program.

Investment Home Characteristics for Government Housing Assistance Programs

» In most major metro areas, the assistance programs require central heat and central air conditioning.

» The home must be in good repair and move-in condition.

» All kitchen appliances must be supplied, including a refrigerator. It is recommended that a washer and dryer also be supplied. A washer and dryer provide more value to a tenant (which translates to higher rent payments). An owner supplied washer and dryer would ensure that there are no installation problems involving electricity or plumbing. A garbage disposal is not required or recommended.

» The house should be safe. Make sure that there are no interior or exterior issues that may affect one's health or well-being.

Other Essential Standards That You Should Adhere To

» Homes should have good curb appeal. Even though there is a surplus of families eligible for rental assistance, a renter is not guaranteed. You are providing more than shelter; you are providing a home for a family that will potentially live there for many years. There needs to be some pride in the property in order for the tenant to call your investment their home. It is also the tenant's choice whether to rent from you or from someone else.

» Try to purchase properties that have a minimum of three bedrooms and two bathrooms. The more bedrooms there are, the higher the monthly rent (four to five bedrooms is ideal). There is more demand for larger homes than smaller ones. Additionally, houses with more bedrooms appreciate and sell faster. Still, these programs will allow one and two bedroom homes, and there are some densely populated areas around the United States where one and two bedroom homes draw unusually high rents.

Expect it to take thirty to sixty days to obtain a quality tenant. A serious investor should be able to financially survive the time it takes to lease the property. If you are in the market for a tenant during inclement weather or during the holidays (Thanksgiving through New Year's Day), it could take up to ninety days to obtain a quality tenant. Make sure you can get through this period when necessary.

Renting Homes in a Soft Rental Market

Many potential investors are hesitant to buy rental homes because they are worried about not having a tenant to offset their mortgage payment and fear owning an empty house. By considering housing assistance programs, you vastly expand the number of potential tenants, even when the rental market is soft or seems oversaturated. Most major areas in the United States have a waiting list of families who are eligible for housing assistance, so there is an almost endless supply of tenants for these types of homes.

Collect Above-Market Rents

Another advantage of government housing assistance programs is the amount of rent paid per home—it is paid according to the size of the family. The larger the family, the higher the rent that is allowed. This is commonly known as the voucher system.

Section 8 pays rents according to a scale that ranges from zero bedrooms (efficiency) to six bedrooms. For example, a family with a four bedroom voucher can have more of their rent paid on a home than a family with a three bedroom voucher. In many cases, the rents offered by Section 8 are much higher than you can obtain through a private rental. Visit www.hud.gov/offices/pih/pha/contacts/index.cfm for more information on Section 8 rents in your city.

Learn the System

If you want your property to be considered by government assisted tenants, the property manager of your PBI team must know the Section 8 process. In general, properties available to eligible families are posted on the Section 8 Web site. However, in many cases, Section 8 families do not own a computer. To remedy this, Section 8 also provides a bulletin board at their headquarters that lists properties available for rent, and it is usually updated every Friday. The list of available homes includes each property's description, address, the number of bedrooms, and contact information. Prospective tenants can choose potential properties based on their vouchers and the number of bedrooms in a home.

Once a tenant is found, the owner (your property manager would typically do this for you) contacts Section 8. A property inspection is then scheduled with a Section 8 inspector. Once the inspection is complete and any necessary repairs are made, you will be told the amount that will be paid for the rental. In some cases, the rent offered by Section 8 may not be acceptable. If this happens, you can still negotiate with Section 8. It is not uncommon to negotiate a rent amount that will satisfy both Section 8 and the property investor. (There are hundreds of Section 8 offices offering rental assistance throughout the country. Each individual office operates independently. The rules and procedures may differ slightly from office to office.)

In general, Section 8 will pay most or all of the monthly rent. If the tenant is responsible for a portion of it—usually around 10 percent—you or your property manager will be responsible for collecting that amount. While this may raise a red flag in your mind, experience has taught me that it is generally positive to have a Section 8 tenant who is required to pay a portion of the rent. Not only will he or she feel a greater sense of ownership over the property, and therefore be more interested in its maintenance, but your property manager can arrange to collect the tenant's portion in person. By physically visiting the property, your manager has an opportunity to inspect the property firsthand at the beginning of each month. This usually will keep you abreast of any repairs or potential problems.

The Stopgaps of Section 8

Depending on whom you talk to, you may hear negative things about Section 8. A common assumption is that the tenant will destroy or devalue the property. Yet I've found there are many successful owners who rent out to Section 8 tenants and are completely satisfied with the results.

In order to be successful with renting to Section 8 tenants, you should be working with a property manager who is thoroughly familiar with housing assistance programs. And there are many stopgaps built into the program to protect the property owner.

For starters, the tenant must be employed to receive Section 8 vouchers. A gainfully employed individual is usually more responsible than someone who does not work. The Section 8 tenant must also take a class to be eligible for the program. Property owners are encouraged to attend the class, too. The class stresses the tenant's responsibilities and the fact that he or she can lose their benefit if the property is not maintained. For many, this could be a substantial loss, so the tenant has a lot at stake.

Finally, when a lease is signed through Section 8, the tenant must list everyone who will occupy the home. This doesn't keep the tenants from taking advantage of the system, but it does discourage them from housing additional people for fear of losing the government's support.

Besides the built-in benefits provided by Section 8 regulations, your property manager has some additional flexibility to protect your investment. The following bits of information are not covered in the Section 8 class, yet are points you should consider.

First, Section 8 does not require a security deposit although asking for one is allowed. My managers have determined that by requiring an upfront security deposit we generally obtain a more responsible tenant. It makes sense that someone who has the ability to pay a deposit is more financially secure and will probably take better care of your home.

Another bit of information that you and your property manager should know is that you do not have to take the first tenant that comes along. There is no automatic assignment of tenants. You are permitted to select the people who will occupy your investment. And just like in the private rental market, you can check the references for a potential tenant.

In many investment circles, investing in qualified Section 8 housing is made to sound like it is more trouble than it is worth, or that it's not glamorous. This is generally the opinion of those who have either never tried it, or who invest for reasons of self-importance and greed. My personal experience, and that of many I know, tells me that providing properties for people who would otherwise never own their own home, in most cases, reaps a reward better than money. Knowing you've made a wise investment that is being subsidized by the government is thrilling, but knowing that you are providing a home for a family who needs one is a pleasure you can't put a price on.

PBI Notes

» Government housing assistance programs. There are opportunities in most areas of the country to lease to tenants who are helped by the government through Section 8.

» It is important to work with a property manager who is experienced in working with Section 8 and Section 8 tenants.

» For more information on government assisted rental programs, go to my Web site at pushbuttoninvesting.com.

PUT YOUR TOE IN TO TEST THE WATER

*"Always do your best.
What you plant now, you will
harvest later."*

Og Mandino

Patience Can Pay Off

When people realize the income potential in real estate using the PBI system, they usually become excited and cannot wait to get started. They want to cash in right away. But in order to be successful in real estate, you must be patient.

A client of mine named Frank had his first investment home under contract. It was under construction and due to be completed in November. Frank was excited and wanted to become an instant millionaire. He had reason to be excited. He had done everything right. He found a property locator, and together they contracted for a home in a highly appreciating area. The area was also ideal for Section 8 rentals.

However, due to government red tape in the form of a moratorium on sewer taps, the completion of Frank's home was delayed. He called me several times in December—a month after the home was supposed to be ready—to complain about the builder's delay.

January came and the home was still not completed. I received another round of calls. Since it was not fun fielding Frank's calls about this construction project delay I had nothing to do with, I followed a hunch and did a little research of my own.

I found that Frank's house had gone up $15,000 in value since he wrote the contract in August. Additionally, he had no mortgage or financial obligation on this asset that was earning money. I called Frank and told him what I discovered. The builder, I reminded him, was obligated to deliver a $150,000 priced home that was currently worth $165,000. In other words, it did not matter how long it took to build—he was making money either way. Besides that, Frank wasn't waiting to move in. He already owned a home that he lived in. I told Frank to be grateful, because he managed to acquire an appreciating asset with no obligation. I told him if it were me, I would be thrilled if it took another six months to complete. The experience taught Frank—and me—that patience can certainly pay off.

Buy One House and See How It Works

Most people who want to start investing in real estate have in mind to dive in headfirst. Convinced it is easy to succeed, they believe they need to immediately build a real estate portfolio.

While there is nothing complicated about investing in real estate, we all have to remember that succeeding is just as easy as failing. If this will be your first time investing, you should start with one house and see how it works out for you. Go through the search process with a property locator, partner with a professional lender, and lease the property or have a manager lease it for you.

Once your first home is acquired, wait a few months before considering another home for investment. Make sure the tenant is paying on time and there are no unforeseen expenses. While it can be stressful to own another property besides the one you live in, remember, to be successful at PBI, it only takes one purchase a year.

Quality, Not Quantity

The ultimate key to being a successful investor is finding the right house. If you find the right house, the rest falls into place. Is it in an area with a high velocity of appreciation? Is it in a safe area? Are the rents in the area above average? Is the house in good repair? Be patient, be diligent, and keep in mind that you make your money when you buy.

After the Dust Settles, Buy Another

A successful PBI strategy is to take care of business one house at a time. Once you have done the research, acquired the property, leased the home, and received rents for a few months, then look into acquiring another property. Often, when you find something that works, you can duplicate it. Buy in the same area, or even in the same neighborhood if it makes sense. You don't need to change a winning strategy, but do remind yourself that you only need to buy one house a year. This is all it takes to create a perpetual, annual cash flow, so don't move too fast.

> *"I attended one of Ron's seminars and was blown away. It is so simple, so logical, and it worked for me."*
>
> Susan Fyvolent
> *Real Estate Attorney*

Try Another Part of Town

Once you acquire a few homes, you may find yourself in an area saturated with investors. Values likely have gone up significantly and it might be time to buy elsewhere. Your PBI team is always aware of these types of changes. When this occurs, there may be another area of town that offers a high velocity of appreciation and high rents at a lower purchase price. Keep your eyes and ears open, and make sure your team is doing the same.

Sometimes an oversaturated area becomes a good catalyst for you to consider other properties. It gives you a reason to buy in a different part of town, which is wise to do because you will have the chance to diversify your real estate holdings. Real estate purchases, like stock and bond investments, can be spread out to reduce risk. There are typically many pocket areas that can be profitable in any given city of a medium to large size.

PBI NOTES

» Patience. Investing in real estate is your choice. Only buy if the property meets the right investing criteria.

» Buy one house and see how it works. Once you get a tenant, enjoy the investment.

» After the dust settles, buy another. Make sure that your new home is leased and the tenant has consistently paid the rent on time before your next purchase.

» Try another part of town. After you buy houses in one area, have your locator watch for other areas that meet the PBI requirements.

16
HAVING THE
RIGHT ATTITUDE

*"He who is not courageous enough to take
risks will accomplish nothing in life."*

Muhammad Ali

Unlucky Charlie

Owning investment property requires the right attitude. Charlie, a client of mine, purchased a property and was acting as his own property manager. He was thrilled about getting a great deal and felt fortunate to have a tenant move in shortly after the purchase. Life was great, and he was looking forward to adding properties to his portfolio.

About a month later, Charlie received a call from his tenant. She made numerous demands for repairs and improvements. She wanted Charlie to install a screen door, change a light fixture to a different style, and carpet one of the rooms. Charlie's heart sank. He didn't know what to do. The house was beautifully rehabilitated and in perfect shape. It didn't need what the tenant was requesting, but he did not want to lose his renter. Charlie felt vulnerable and was essentially at his tenant's mercy.

Unfortunately, this scenario is all too common when it comes to investment property. To avoid this unenviable situation and succeed as your own property manager, you must adopt the right attitude. You must take control from the outset.

You purchased a property that you are proud of. It is in great shape and there are no repairs needed. You are providing a home that anyone would be proud to live in. Your tenants should feel privileged to reside there. If they do not feel that way, they might be the wrong tenants.

But let's assume you've already accepted the tenants' deposit and they have moved in. What do you do to ensure that you don't end up in Charlie's shoes? A successful property owner/manager sets a precedent upfront. Tell your tenants you are happy to provide them with a beautiful home that is in excellent condition. In doing so, you expect that the rent will be paid on the first of each month and that any legitimate repairs be brought to your immediate attention.

While this won't necessarily alter the personality of an overbearing or overanxious tenant who has already signed a contract, being tactfully assertive from the beginning will help weed out unnecessary requests. If you are assertive when interviewing prospective tenants, this is even better.

A professional attitude will let potential tenants know that you place a high value on your property and are particular about who lives there. Knowing this, they will generally hold a healthy respect for you and your house. They will want to protect your property by caring for it properly. Your pride of ownership will be conveyed to the tenant and the tenant will in turn be proud to live there.

There are additional actions you can take that will help you set up your landlord/tenant relationship to succeed. First, always give them a thorough tour of the property. Point out the improvements and upgrades that were made. Explain the systems (heating, air conditioning, and burglar alarm) and demonstrate how to use them if necessary. You would be surprised at how many people do not know how to use a thermostat.

Then, when your tenants move in, provide them with an initial supply of garbage can liners. Get them in the habit of taking out the garbage regularly. Show them the yard and explain how often the grass needs to be mowed. Train these people to be good tenants. Set them up to succeed, too.

If Charlie had enlisted a similar attitude about his property from the start, he would not have found himself in the sticky situation he was forced to confront. When we spoke, he needed advice on how to handle his demanding tenant, so I referred him to one of my property managers.

The manager taught Charlie how to confront the tenant in an assertive and professional manner. He told him the following: "Explain to her, 'You moved into my beautiful home that needed no repairs. What I do in a case where improvements are requested is charge a $50 service fee to come out to the property. If there are legitimate repairs needed, we will repair the property and waive the fee. If you want carpeting, a new light fixture, or any other improvement, there will be a $50 service charge to come out and give you an estimate. If you choose to have the improvement done, the service charge will go towards the cost of the improvement. We expect payment promptly upon completion of the work you request.'"

After hearing this suggestion, Charlie was blown away. My experienced property manager was confident and to the point. It made sense to Charlie, and he proceeded to say the same thing to the tenant. In response, the tenant backed off on her unnecessary requests, and after two years has not given Charlie any further trouble.

The property that you buy is your investment. You need to protect it by setting a precedent. Namely, this requires having the right attitude and remaining in control of the situation. Set your relationships up for success and you will continue to enjoy the benefits of investing.

PBI NOTES

» Attitude. You need to be clear and concise. You can avoid being taken advantage of by having the right attitude.

Management
Checklist

*"What I do is prepare myself
until I know I can do what I have to do."*

Joe Namath

Proper management and control of your investment property is critical. As the number of investment homes that you own increases, you or your property manager must regularly make sure that everything is in order. I have compiled a checklist for you to use that will ensure proper maintenance and upkeep of the property, as well as a watchful eye on the tenant. (This can also be used when looking at properties for purchase.)

Exterior of the Home

√ The roof must be sound and free of leaks.

√ Exterior walls must be in good shape and have no paint that is peeling.

√ If the home has gutters, they must be clog-free.

√ Windows must be workable and have locks on them.

√ Exterior doors and crawl space doors must be able to stand up to frequent use and have workable locks on them.

√ Windows that are designed to be opened must have screens in them.

√ Any stairs with more than four steps must have handrails, and porches must have guardrails. (The building code requirements may vary from state to state.)

√ The exterior should be free of trash and garbage. This includes the lawn, crawl space, and any other area on the outside of the home.

√ The outside should be well-maintained, with the lawn and shrubs properly trimmed. (Once the tenant moves in, the agreement as set forth in the lease will dictate who maintains the landscape.)

√ There should be sufficient ground cover. Many times, grass does not exist because it became a high traffic area. This is a home that you are providing for someone. It should look and feel like one.

Mechanics and Systems of the Home

√ All systems should be in good repair and operational. This includes all appliances, the heating and air conditioning systems, and the hot water tank.

√ All utilities must be on upon inspection by the tenant and any rental assistance official. This allows for testing any appliance or system.

√ There cannot be any uncovered electrical outlets, panels, or exposed wires.

√ Systems must be up to code. This includes all plumbing, electrical, and heating/air conditioning systems. Building codes vary from state to state. Your home inspector should be able to confirm whether your property complies.

Interior of the Home

√ Each bedroom must have a closet and a window that operates properly.

√ Each bedroom must have the use of a bathroom that can be accessed without going through another bedroom.

√ Bathroom doors must have properly working locks.

√ The walls must be clean and free of holes or any other damage.

√ All carpeting must be clean and free of holes or tears.

√ Smoke alarms must be installed on each floor of the home.

√ No evidence of animal or insect infestation, mold/mildew, sewer odor, or gases such as propane/natural gas should be present.

PBI Notes

» The home that you invest in must meet certain requirements. By knowing that the home is in good working order, you should be able to avoid most major repairs for the next five to seven years.

» For a reprint of the lists in this section, go to my Web site at pushbuttoninvesting.com.

EXPECTATIONS

*"Ideas are the beginning points
for all fortunes."*

Napoleon Hill

Property Owner's Expectations of a
Property Manager

» The manager must be able to lease the property quickly.

» Good communication with the tenant is important.

» It is up to the manager to see that the property is maintained.

» You must be notified if repairs are needed on the property.

» Your phone calls are to be returned in a relatively quick manner.

» A report to you is required at least quarterly.

Property Owner's Expectations of Tenants

» Tenants must be reliable when they need to meet contractors or inspectors at the house.

» Rent must be paid on time.

» A renter must be stable. (A stable tenant resides in the home for more than two years. This cuts down on the expense of new paint and fix-up every time a tenant is replaced.)

» Renting to smaller families is preferred (fewer occupants mean less wear and tear).

» A "no pets" policy is preferable (but not mandatory).

» Two income families are preferred. This makes for a more financially responsible tenant.

» Good credit is a must.

» The utilities are to be transferred into the tenants' name immediately upon moving in.

Property Manager's Goals and Expectations When Working with Tenants

» Always be available to the tenant as a resource whenever there is an issue involving the property.

» Be involved and talk with the tenants. In this way, you will know what's going on.

» Respond quickly to questions and the need for repairs. This is also the tenant's home, and he or she should feel at home there.

» Conduct regular, non-intrusive visits. This tells tenants that you value the property and them as tenants.

» Follow up immediately if the rent check is late.

» Maintain a list of quality contacts for electricians and plumbers.

» Routinely inspect the property when a repair is requested. If the damage was caused by the tenant, the tenant should expect to pay for it. (A property manager should have moderate repair skills, which, in many cases, can save a service charge by a licensed, professional repairman.)

> *"You have the deal down for passive investors like me. I never knew that investment property ownership could be so simple and easy."*
>
> *Dave Vogel*
> *asset manager*

How to Make Routine Inspections and What to Watch For

The tenant should be notified from the start that your property manager has the right to inspect and maintain the property. To be safe, this should be written into the lease and then explained so there are no surprises. The following are items your property manager should watch for when conducting these inspections.

Change the air filter monthly. Routine maintenance allows the property manager to enter the home. If the tenant is in, the property manager can ask if there are any problems. Your manager should always ask or look for standing water. Standing water or water stains on the ceiling can be the start of a major problem. If the property manager is not checking in routinely, you will eventually find out about any problems, sometimes after it's too late.

Check the kitchen sink for leaks. Underneath the sink is another area where water may accumulate.

Check for insect or pest infestation. This problem can occur due to an accumulation of old food or garbage, and can eventually affect the structure of your home. If your manager notices infestation, the causes should be explained and a solution politely suggested.

Are there any signs of pets? Many leases do not allow pets, but that is ultimately up to you. A water or food bowl on the floor is a sign of a pet.

Check underneath the home and in the yard. Many times, people discard old mattresses and trash under the house. It is not a place for storage and should be kept clear of debris. An accumulation of discarded items under the house can attract pests. The property manager should also observe if the tenants are keeping the yard up. Is it mowed? Most leases require the tenants to do so.

Inspect the utility meters. The concern is not about the tenants' use of electricity or gas, but whether the bills are being paid. If a meter has a lock on it, that's a sign of the utility being shut off for lack of payment.

If your property manager notices anything that affects the integrity of the home that the tenants are not complying with, they should bring it to the tenants' attention in a professional manner. The property manager will advise the tenant that he or she will be back to see that it has been remedied. That is important. If the tenants know that the manager does not follow up, they may ignore future requests.

As you begin to put PBI to work for you, you may find other items that necessitate routine check-ups. However, those I've mentioned above are the most common and should not be ignored. It should also be noted, before we move on, that no matter what sort of inspection routine you implement, you should strive to not become a nuisance to your tenants. They have a right to their privacy. Any inspections to make sure the house is maintained and safe need to be legitimate.

Never forget your overarching goals, which are to maintain a beautiful, well-functioning home and keep satisfied, quality tenants. If you accomplish the first goal with tact, respect, and excellence, the second goal seems, in most cases, to happen as a natural matter of course. Once you and your team become pros at accomplishing your goals for each home, you will probably find that investing in real estate is one of the easiest and most pleasurable endeavors you can pursue.

Now, if you're ready, let's talk about how to get started with Push Button Investing today by building your PBI team.

PBI NOTES

» Whether you are using a property manager or managing the property yourself, you must understand what to look for.

» For a reprint of the lists in this section, go to my Web site at pushbuttoninvesting.com

PART FIVE

BEGINNING PUSH BUTTON INVESTING

BUILDING YOUR PBI TEAM

"Hire the best people and then delegate."

Carl A. Tabor

Finding a Lender

The lender you are looking for is typically a mortgage loan officer who specifically knows about lending to investors. Mortgage rules and guidelines for real estate investment lending are different from those for lending to people who occupy their homes. Sometimes it is difficult to qualify for an investment property mortgage without a lease to offset the payments. An experienced mortgage lender can assist Push Button Investors in almost any situation.

Here are a few places to look for a lender:

» The mortgage lender whom you used to finance your primary home

» A referral from your property locator

» A referral from a friend who has multiple homes

» A referral from a trustworthy Certified Public Accountant (CPA) who works with a mortgage lender

It is best to talk to lenders before proposing the PBI opportunity to them. Here are a few interview questions:

» Are you familiar with investment lending?

» What percentage of your loans is for investment homes versus owner occupied homes?

» Can you facilitate mortgages for investors who have no property investment experience?

» Can you lend to investors who might not qualify without a lease?

» Do you offer 95 percent to 100 percent financing on investment property?*

» Do you own investment property? How long have you owned your properties?

» Do you have references?

*The question regarding 95-100 percent financing is somewhat of a trick question. Many lenders offer very low down payment mortgages on investment property.

But a caring lender knows that investment lending with low down payments—less than 10 percent—carries higher mortgage rates. In addition, a lower down payment produces a larger mortgage, which makes the house payment more costly. Remember, successful PBI investors want to have a positive monthly cash flow, or at least break even. As the mortgage payments rise, breaking even becomes more difficult. There are, of course, situations where it makes sense to get maximum financing, but in most cases it is not advised. A quality lender will understand this and make it known to you.

Finding a Property Locator

The property locator is generally an experienced, licensed real estate agent. He or she must be able to find properties in areas that have a high velocity of appreciation. Additionally, the properties must be in areas that lease easily, both privately and through government housing assistance programs.

Here are a few people who may be or know of a successful property locator:

» Real estate agents you trust

» Property managers that your friends or family use

» Builders

» Another real estate investor

» A mortgage lender

» A CPA who has clients that invest in real estate

When seeking out a property locator, here are a few interview questions you should ask:

» Do you own residential rental property? How many properties do you own?

» Who do you know that owns residential rental property?

» In which area of town are the properties located?

» Do you sell or have you sold more than one property in each area?

» Who manages the properties?

» What will each property be worth in three to five years? Why do you think so?

» Are the areas of town in which you sell investment properties easily rentable?

» What percentage of local leases are private versus government sponsored?

» Do you have references?

These questions will reveal the experience the potential locator has with investment real estate. Do not be discouraged if the person you interview is not the right fit. He or she may know other experienced people who can either locate properties or refer people to you who can. Your goal is to find a locator who has the same investment standards that you do—a high velocity of appreciation and a good market for rentals. You may have to interview a few people before you find the right one.

Finding a Property Manager

The property manager is a vital part of your team. This person is the key member who takes the hassle out of owning property. Personally, I would not be a real estate investor if I had to manage my own properties.

When searching for the right person, here are a few people who might make excellent property managers:

» Professional property managers

» Real estate investors who manage their own property

» Apartment maintenance professionals

» Rehabbers

» Builders

» Property locators (some locators make great managers)

When interviewing potential managers, here are the questions you should ask:

» Do you currently own and manage your own investment properties? (If the answer is no, you may not want to continue with this person. An exception might be a manager who has owned properties in the past.)

» How many properties do you own?

» How many properties do you manage?

» What is your fee? (A fair payment is a one-time fee equaling the first month's rent for locating a tenant and then 7-10 percent of the rent paid monthly.)

» Are you familiar with government housing assistance programs?

» Do you have experience with Section 8 rentals?

» Do you do your own repairs?

» Do you have a crew or a source of contacts for major repairs?

» How do you communicate with your property owners? How often?

» Do you have references?

Ultimately, the property manager is your main link to your investment for the years that you own the property. You need to have a high degree of trust in this person and a strong working relationship. And while you will work more regularly with your property manager, every member of your team is important. You cannot afford a weak link.

It is my belief that each person on your Push Button Investing team must have experience in owning investment property. In this way, they can know firsthand what you are trying to accomplish. Working with fellow investors does cause some concern, however. I have come across many first-time PBI investors who are worried that property locators will keep the "good" properties for themselves and only offer the leftover, less profitable properties to their investors. New PBI investors are also concerned that property managers will take better care of their own properties and choose the better tenants for themselves.

While these are valid concerns, good PBI locators and managers are fully aware of the needs of their clients. They know that wrong advice or actions will hurt their business. They also understand that it only takes one property a year to be successful with the PBI model, and there are plenty of great properties available.

Quality locators and managers realize that their personal real estate investments make up a small portion of their earnings. They know that in order to keep working for qualified investors, they need to meet and exceed the investors' goals. Their job is not only to service investors but make them so successful that they will be referred to other investors.

A word on potentially negative experiences with PBI: While every entrepreneurial endeavor carries with it an element of risk, the PBI model is not on the higher end of the risk spectrum. In many instances, we already know and trust people whom we can hire for our team. In my case, I already knew Ben. He was a client for whom I originally funded a home loan. We trusted each other and had a good working relationship. When it came time for me to hire a property manager, the choice was easy.

Ben was a hard worker, and having been successful at investing in and managing properties for himself, understood what it took to maintain a profitable investment property.

Chances are good that you—directly or indirectly, through a friend or family member—know hard-working, trustworthy people with investment experience who would be great candidates for the three positions on your PBI team. If you've purchased a home before, you already know a potential PBI lender. If you found that home through a Realtor, you already know a potential PBI locator. If you know someone who owns investment property, you probably know an individual with property management experience. These people may not be the perfect fit for your team, and you may not know them that well, but they are a good place to start.

For additional contacts, send out an e-mail to your close friends and family members. Explain what you are doing and ask who they know who could be an ideal fit for your investment team. You will likely be surprised at how many potential team members you end up with.

In the unlikely event that you have absolutely no leads for people to join your PBI team, don't worry—you still have the resources to find the right people. The questions you previously read are for this purpose. And once you gain confidence in the PBI process, hiring the right people will become second nature. I still utilize the services of many of the people with whom I originally began investing. Trust me; it's not difficult to get people excited about an opportunity that is good for everyone involved.

> *"Your book, which is on a heavily written topic, compelled me to invest in real estate."*
>
> Brent Cole
> *writer*

PBI NOTES

» The easiest way to be successful with PBI investing is to hire a PBI team. The PBI team knows the property, finance, and management criteria needed for you to be successful.

» Go to my Web site at www.pushbuttoninvesting.com for more information on PBI teams.

TAX ADVANTAGES OF REAL ESTATE INVESTING

"Keeping a little ahead of business is one of the secrets of business."

Charles M. Schwab

Real estate is one of the most tax friendly investments around. In many cases, you can lower or even avoid taxes when you buy, hold, and sell real estate. However, the U.S. tax code can be complicated. It is important to consult your tax advisor before making decisions that involve tax reporting.

Mortgage Interest

We have all heard that Uncle Sam helps us make our mortgage payments. The fact is that only the interest portion of your mortgage payment is tax deductible. But this is still very helpful in the early years of your mortgage.

If you have an interest-only mortgage, then 100 percent of your payment is tax deductible. The actual savings that you receive depends on your tax bracket, but all savings are advantageous. If you are in the 30 percent tax bracket, after taxes, your mortgage payment is discounted by 30 percent. If the interest portion of your payment was $1,000, your tax deduction would be $300. That makes your effective payment equivalent to $700 a month.

No matter what type of property you own, the interest is deductible. The property can be your primary residence, second home, or investment property. In this way, the government is helping you buy your investment real estate.

> *"You did a great job
> simplifying the process."*
>
> Gina Garcia
> stay-at-home mom

Discount Points

When purchasing real estate, there are usually closing costs. The discount points and origination fee portion of the closing costs are generally tax deductible in the year the property is acquired. These fees allow for a better interest rate and are therefore considered prepaid interest, which is tax deductible. In many cases, these fees are paid by the seller as an incentive to buy the property. However, the fees are only tax deductible to the buyer, whether they are paid by the seller or the buyer.

Depreciation

Depreciation on real estate is a noncash deduction on your investment. Depreciation is considered only on the structure, not the land. Essentially, the structure is going to devalue over time because of the wear and tear from renters living in the home. To calculate depreciation, the value of the structure is divided up over a certain number of years.

For example, if you had a structure valued at $100,000 and depreciated it over twenty-five years, your annual depreciation would be $4,000. That $4,000 may be used as a property expense on your tax return. It does not cost you anything, but it enables you to report less profit. Your tax advisor will help you determine how to calculate depreciation based on your particular situation. In any case, this tax advantage is something you should not overlook.

Capital Gains

A married couple is allowed to accumulate up to $500,000 in tax-exempt profits on gains realized from the sale of their primary residence during their lifetime. A single person may accumulate exempt gains of up to $250,000. If you convert a primary home into a rental property, you might be able to benefit from the same tax treatment. The current tax law allows this benefit if the property was a primary home in two of the past five years. No other investment, such as stocks or bonds, allows this type of flexibility.

Profits on investment property that was never a primary residence are subject to a tax called capital gains. These tax rates have historically been lower than rates on ordinary income, for those who sell property they have held for at least one year. If you are dead set on selling an investment home in less than a year to turn a quick profit, consult your tax advisor first.

1031 Tax-Free Exchange

Imagine if you could accumulate a lifetime of capital gains on the sale of your real estate investments and avoid paying taxes. You could amass hundreds of thousands, or even millions of dollars in profits, and not pay a dime. This can be done with a 1031 tax-free exchange.

The IRS allows you to use the proceeds from the sale of investment property to purchase like-kind property without paying taxes. The rules are somewhat flexible. If you sell a property, you can wait up to six months before closing on a new property. You do, however, have to identify the property that you will be purchasing within six weeks. Every time you sell a property, the proceeds may be rolled into one or more new properties without tax consequences.

There are simple guidelines and procedures you will need to follow. Before selling a property using a 1031 tax-free exchange, consult with your tax advisor or a reputable exchange intermediary. It is important to understand that the 1031 tax-free exchange is actually a way to defer (not eliminate) taxes on your gain. By having a well-thought-out strategy, you could utilize this tax benefit to your advantage.

Real Estate Related Expenses

The two largest expenses in owning real estate investments are interest and depreciation. Other expenses may include repairs, insurance, and management fees. They are all expenses that may offset profits. The lower the reported profits, the less tax liability you will have. If you have extra cash at the end of the year, it may be better to make repairs before year end in order to lower your profits and thus your tax liability.

Many investors own multiple properties. While some of their properties may be profitable, others may lose them money. Often, their losses will offset the profits on their gains. The shrewd investor will manage his or her properties in such a fashion that the entire real estate portfolio will break even or show a small loss. In some cases, depending on your tax bracket, a loss on your real estate schedule may even offset your income from employment or other sources.

Real estate investing offers quite favorable tax treatment in comparison to other types of investments. You can write off the financing used to acquire your property. You can expense items required to maintain your property. You can expense depreciation but it does not cost you anything. You can offset profitable properties with unprofitable properties. You can sell and not pay taxes by using a 1031 tax-free exchange. Investing in real estate offers highly favorable tax treatment, great profits, and the benefit of helping others less fortunate than you live in quality housing.

PBI NOTES

» Investing in real estate is one of the most tax-friendly investments that you can make. When considering your tax liabilities, it is important to get expert advice from your tax advisor.

» To learn more about 1031 tax-free exchanges, go to my Web site at pushbuttoninvesting.com

Putting It All Together

"We make a living by what we get.
But we make a life by what we give."
Winston Churchill

Pursuing Push Button Investing

You are now ready to pursue real estate investing. The important thing is to carefully follow the steps of the PBI system. Remember, you do not have to buy immediately. All it takes is one purchase a year, and each purchase should comply with the PBI parameters we have described thus far.

Interview and choose a PBI team in whom you can have the utmost confidence. Once you successfully do this, you are ready to purchase your first home. Be picky. The right house in the right location is the key. Then, with one home in your portfolio, observe your team. Make sure they are working in your best interest. Does your locator follow up with market changes? Are all members communicating with you? Are they keeping you updated on what is happening in the neighborhood? Are values increasing? Are there other areas that you should pursue in the future?

Is your property manager giving you quarterly reports about your investment? Are your tenants paying rent on time? What kind of housekeepers are they? Are your tenants keeping up with the landscaping? Does it appear there are more occupants than the number the tenants indicated on the lease? These are the types of questions your PBI team should be able to readily answer.

Today, I work with several PBI investors. Ironically, the biggest problem that I find is the simplicity of the system. This method of owning property excites new investors. Their first reaction is to buy up properties rapidly. While a more seasoned investor might do this, it's not advisable for people just beginning.

Real estate, like most investments, has risks. To be successful with PBI, you only need to purchase one quality home a year. In other words, take your time. You will create wealth for yourself if you follow the system. As you accumulate properties, you will gain more experience. By limiting your properties to five—the amount of properties owned at any one time—you will have a manageable portfolio. Then, once you have more experience, you might want to buy two investment homes per year.

Some of my clients observed their PBI team members so much that they became proficient in locating and managing their own properties. This is up to you. For many, this is very enjoyable and an easy way to maintain full understanding of what is happening with their properties. The lesson here is that experience takes many of the unknowns out of investing.

Personally, I still prefer my properties to be managed for me. I have owned properties for many years and employ the services of a PBI team. My belief is that I can own real estate with minimal effort on my part. It's like buying a stock mutual fund with one exception: I have personally interviewed the person who locates the stock. I personally know the manager of the stock as well. Additionally, I know that these people who are watching my investment are investors themselves. They are in the same boat. They too are interested in preserving and growing the equity in their properties. My properties are generally in the same area of town as theirs, so we celebrate similar successes. Finally, I have a personal relationship with these people who handle my valuable assets. This is rarely the case when investing in mutual funds.

I understand that finding the right people for a PBI team poses a challenge for some. Investors have come to me from time to time and expressed that they could not find the right people. They are interested in investing but are not confident enough to take the first step and create a quality team. In many cases, we have been able to match investors with existing teams. Today, we have investors from as far away as California buying property in Atlanta, Georgia. They are confident in the system and are thrilled to have the opportunity to invest with an experienced team.

Soon there will be trained PBI teams throughout the country. This will open up more opportunities for people who want to invest in their hometowns. The important thing to remember, however, is that as long as the property has a high velocity of appreciation and can be easily rented, it does not matter where the property is located. You do not need to live close by. For many, the experience of those on their team provides plenty of confidence in their investments.

Whether you decide to do it all yourself, hire a team, or use the services of an existing PBI team, now is the time to invest. There are always great investment opportunities somewhere—often right under our noses. You will begin to see them when you learn how to look for them, or when you know whom to hire to look for you.

> *"I highly recommend Ron Draluck's Push Button Investing System. It is the real estate investment 'easy button.'"*
>
> *Wendy Bear*
> *insurance agent*

Now is your chance to begin. The PBI system has taken the fear out of investing. You can own investment property with no painting, hammering, tenant phone calls, or contract work. If you so choose, all you need to do is push the buttons on a calculator and watch your real estate wealth grow. I hope you will give it a try.

Profitability and Humanity

A final word about success: Many people define it as dollars and profitability. If they become rich and can afford nice things, they consider themselves to be successful. The truth is, many of the same people only appear successful. They may "look like a million bucks" but they are miserable. Melancholy millionaires, I see it all the time.

As a real estate investor, you can amass hundreds of thousands, even millions of dollars, and still have no meaning in your life. If this is possible, then it makes sense for us to write a deeper definition of success, one that isn't solely dependent on our financial gains and losses. Eventually, we all understand this.

A sense of success may be achieved by helping others. This is why volunteering is so enriching. Some of the happiest people we meet from day to day are not financially well-off. Essentially, they find fulfillment in helping others be successful, even if it earns them little or no money.

The beauty of Push Button Investing is that it offers both the financial stability we seek and the personal fulfillment we often lack in our nine-to-five jobs. I'll admit, when I first got started in real estate investing, it was all about the money. I was looking to create wealth for myself and my family. I succeeded in doing that. Yet as my real estate portfolio grew, I found that I was doing more than creating personal wealth: I was providing shelter for my tenants. I was providing quality housing for people in areas of town where quality housing was not common.

In today's society, where the average person is quick to criticize or complain, it is rare to receive a thank-you. As a PBI investor, I began receiving many thank-yous and compliments from the people who were renting my properties. Not only were the tenants excited to move into one of my houses, some of the government housing assistance employees complimented me on the quality of my homes. I realized that I had obtained a reputation for providing a clean, quality home for people who, in some instances, had never lived in anything half as nice. As a result, I not only quickly leased my homes, I also had tenants who were appreciative of my work.

Through Push Button Investing, I achieved financial stability and continue to receive personal enrichment. In an era of competition and corporate control, this simple investment strategy gave me something most jobs can't or won't. It gave me—and still gives me—professional success and personal significance. Few opportunities can make such a claim. I hope you will decide to take advantage of this one. I truly believe you'll be glad you did.

> *"In over a decade of working with real estate experts, I've never come across something as simple and straightforward as Ron Draluck's Push Button Investing system.*
> *It shortens the investment learning curve to almost nothing."*
>
> Brent Cole
> *writer*

PBI NOTES

» We have all heard stories of how people succeeded in real estate. This is not a get-rich-quick scheme. The PBI system is a proven method for creating wealth through real estate. Anyone can succeed, but first you must begin.

» To find out how to begin investing using the PBI system, go to my Web site at pushbuttoninvesting.com

APPENDIX

Investing Terms

Amortization—Amortization refers to the traditional type of home mortgage. A typical amortization period is thirty years. A loan amortized for thirty years means that it will be paid off over that same period of time. An amortized mortgage is made up of principal and interest. Every time a payment is made, the principal amount owed is reduced.

Annuity—An annuity is a predictable, consistent payment of money that usually lasts for a number of years. Annuities are common insurance investments. In real estate, a properly designed system of buying and selling can create a consistent, annual cash flow that is similar to an annuity.

Appreciation—Appreciation is the increase in an asset's value over time. A home bought for $100,000 may appreciate to $135,000 in five years. The actual appreciation over those years was 35 percent, or $35,000.

Capital Gains—A capital gain is the profit that an investor makes when he or she sells an asset. A capital gain can be made when stocks, bonds, or real estate is sold. Capital gains are taxable. It is important to consult with your tax advisor to determine how your capital gain is treated when filing your tax return.

Cash Flow—Cash flow is the monthly rent you receive, minus the cost of the mortgage payment, management fees, and any other expense that occurs. Having money left over after expenses is positive cash flow, which is ideal. In this way, owning a property is similar to running a small business.

Combined Loan to Value (CLTV)—Sometimes it makes sense for a real estate investor to acquire a property with two mortgages. A typical example is to obtain a first mortgage for 80 percent of the sale price, and a second mortgage for 10 percent of the sale price, for a total combined loan to value (CLTV) of 90 percent. By breaking the financing into two parts, the investor will be able to avoid the added monthly expense of private mortgage insurance (PMI).

Depreciation—Real estate will naturally suffer wear and

tear over the years. Theoretically, at some point your home will suffer enough wear and tear so that the value of the structure is zero. Depreciation is the estimate of how much your structure (home) decreases in value annually. This dollar figure is not paid out to anyone, however the U.S. tax system allows investors to use depreciation as an expense. You may have a positive cash flow but be able to show a loss after you subtract depreciation from the profits. This is a great tax advantage of investing in real estate.

Dividends—Dividends are generally associated with owning stock in a corporation. Many corporations distribute income to their stockholders on a regular basis. This income is referred to as dividends. Investors who own real estate can achieve a similar cash distribution when they have properties that create cash flow.

Equity Stock Pile—A real estate investor with appreciated properties, who has deferred their capital gains by rolling them into new investment properties, has built up an equity stockpile. Their profits are in their real estate and may be realized when sold.

Financial Freedom—A successful PBI investor who can pay their expenses with a perpetual, annual cash flow has achieved financial freedom.

Fixed Rate Mortgage—A fixed rate mortgage is the most common type of loan used in acquiring real estate. The rate and payment never change. A fixed rate mortgage has the highest rate because it is guaranteed for up to thirty years.

Hybrid Mortgage—A hybrid mortgage combines a fixed rate with an adjustable rate mortgage. These mortgages typically cover a thirty-year timespan. They are fixed for the first few years and usually adjust annually after the fixed period. The fixed period may be for one, three, five, seven, or ten years. The shorter the fixed period, the lower the interest rate. The fixed period on a one-year adjustable is lower than the fixed period of a three-year adjustable, which is lower than a five-year adjustable, and so on. Investors who plan to hold their properties for five years might choose to obtain a five-year adjustable rate mortgage because the pricing may be superior to a fixed rate mortgage.

Interest-Only—Payments on an interest-only loan have no principal payment reductions. If the borrower chooses to never pay principal, the mortgage balance will never be paid off. Many investors choose an interest-only loan because the payments are typically the lowest. With a lower monthly payment, they can more easily achieve a cash flow, even in a higher interest rate environment. Most interest-only loans have a feature that requires the principal to be paid beginning in the eleventh year.

Leveraging—Leveraging is a way to acquire assets using other people's money. By obtaining a mortgage, you may only need to pay 10 percent of the purchase price from your own funds. Your mortgage will cover the remaining 90 percent. By leveraging, you reap the benefits of the entire investment (100 percent) while putting up only 10 percent yourself. In other words, you make money on 100 percent of the value of the property while investing 10 percent of its value.

Loan to Value (LTV)—Loan to value is the percentage of monies borrowed. It is the mortgage amount divided by the price paid for the property. If a borrower mortgages $80,000 on a property that costs $100,000, they are borrowing 80 percent ($80,000/$100,000 = 80 percent). A borrower who obtains an 80 percent loan to value is making a 20 percent down payment.

Perpetual, Annual Cash Flow—A real estate investor who consistently buys and sells property may realize a profit from a sale on an annual basis. If the investor maintains this system, he or she will have created a perpetual, annual cash flow.

Portfolio—Stock portfolios most commonly consist of a collection of corporate stocks held by one investor. A real estate investor may have a collection of investment properties in their portfolio. By building a portfolio, the investor can lower his or her risk by averaging the profits and losses among a number of investments.

Tax Deductible Expenses—Most of the expenses involved in owning real estate are tax deductible. Rental income minus tax deductible expenses equals profit. Typical expenses include interest on the mortgage, property taxes, home insurance, management fees, repairs, and depreciation.

Velocity of Appreciation—The speed at which a property grows over time. House "A" may rise in value by $50,000 in eight years. House "B" may increase in value by $50,000 in five years. House "B" has a higher velocity of appreciation. A smart investor chooses properties with the highest velocity of appreciation possible.

1031 Tax-Free Exchange—Investors who profit from the sale of property do not want to pay taxes on their capital gains. A 1031 tax-free exchange is a way to defer taxes when capital gains are achieved. Essentially, the proceeds from the sale of a property are rolled into a new property without tax consequences. While an investor can potentially sell properties for a profit and never pay taxes on the gains, there are specific guidelines to follow when utilizing this strategy. Consult your tax advisor for advice on how to set up an exchange.

FOOTNOTES

1. According to the Joint Economic Study Committee's findings in April 2000. Additional findings from this study can be found at http://www.house.gov/jec/tax/stock/stock.htm.

2. The 6.4 percent statistic that I used came from the article "The Hundred Major Markets." CNN Money.com, May 12, 2005.

3. A collaborative economic study by David Berson, David Lereah, Paul Merski, Frank Nothaft, and David Seiders. "Over the Next 10 Years Home Ownership to Rise." *Originator Times*, January 10, 2005, 1-2.

4. The Kiplinger Washington Editors, "Housing Market." *The Kiplinger Letter*, February 18, 2005, Volume 82, No. 7, 1.

5. Christopher Palmieri, Ann Therese Palmer, and Dean Foust, "After the Housing Boom: What the coming slowdown means for the economy—and you" (cover story) *BusinessWeek*, April 11, 2005, 80-86.

6. Christopher Palmieri, Ann Therese Palmer and Dean Foust, "After the Housing Boom: What the coming slowdown means for the economy—and you" (cover story) *BusinessWeek*, April 11, 2005, 80-86.

About the Author

Ron Draluck is the founder of the Push Button Investing™ System (PBI). He has been a real estate investor for more than twenty-five years. He is a residential mortgage lender, speaker, and gives seminars on creating wealth through home ownership.

Ron has integrated his vast knowledge of real estate investing with mortgage lending to create the PBI System, which has proven to produce a 350 percent return over a five-year period in an average real estate market. There are many ways to profit from real estate, but Ron prefers to use his proven method to achieve a consistent gain.

An Atlanta native, Ron currently lives in Dunwoody, Georgia with his wife, Bonnie, and two sons, Mark and Ross. He earned a BA from Tulane University and an MBA, with a major in finance, from Georgia State University.

More information about Ron and his services can be found at:

www.pushbuttoninvesting.com
info@pushbuttoninvesting.com

Push Button Investing, Inc.
P.O. Box 889354
Atlanta, GA 30356

Order Form

For additional copies of *Push Button Investing in Real Estate,* please fill out the following information or visit the publisher's Web site:

www.ReadingUp.com

Discounts are available for bulk orders and to bookstores, libraries, and other retailers.

Fax orders:	(231)929-1993
Telephone orders:	(231)929-1999
E-mail orders:	Orders@BookMarketingSolutions.com
Postal orders:	BMS
	10300 E. Leelanau Court
	Traverse City, MI 49684

~~~~~~

Please send _____ **copies of** *Push Button Investing in Real Estate.* I understand that I may return any of them for a full refund–for any reason, no questions asked.

Name: _____

Address: _____

City: _____ State: _____ Zip: _____

E-mail address: _____

Phone (in case we need to contact you) _____

Sales Tax: Please add 6% for products being shipped to Michigan addresses.

Shipping by air:
US: $5.00 for the first book and $0.50 for each additional book.
International: $10.00 for the first book and $5.00 for each additional book (estimate).

TOTAL $ _____

Payment: Check   Money Order
Credit Card: Visa   MasterCard   Discover   AmEx

Card Number: _____

Name on Card: _____ Exp. Date: ____/___

Disclaimer

Real estate investing may carry some degree of risk. Before investing in real estate you should carefully consider the risks. The Push Button Investing System is designed to introduce a real estate investment system that has been successful in the past. There is no guaranty of future performance. Push Button Investing, Inc., Ron Draluck, any affiliated Push Button Investing team member, and the publisher specifically disclaim any liability, loss, or risk which is incurred as a consequence, directly or indirectly, of the use and application of any of the contents and methods of this system.

This book is not intended to provide personalized legal, accounting, financial, or investment advice. Readers are encouraged to seek the counsel of competent professionals with regards to these matters as interpretation of the law, proper accounting procedures, financial planning, and investment strategies.